D0818115

Trip Around the World
Quilts

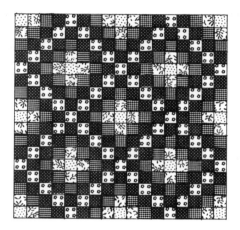

Also by the authors
The Lone Star Quilt Handbook

Trip Around the World

Quilts

a new approach

Blanche Young & Helen Young

Acknowledgements

Our heartfelt thanks to the many people that generously contributed their time and talents during the preparation of this book; to our students for allowing us to photograph their quilts; to Lee Karjala for photographing the quilts so beautifully; to Monette Utz, Annette Cardinal, and Doris Crutchfield for their help; and to Wendy Dodge for the wonderful things she made just for us.

We are grateful for the constant encouragement we received from Gail Giberson, Diana Leone, and Karey Bresenhan. A special thanks to Lynette Bingham, editor and typist, and Donna Tucker, photo stylist and artist, for their contributions. The cooperation from our family and support from husband/father, Dallas, is greatly appreciated.

Published by Young Publications, Box 925, Oak View, California 93022

Printed by The Ink Spot, Ontario, California.
Typesetting by Tech Graphics, Garden Grove, California
Photographs by Lee Karjala
Diagrams and illustrations by Helen Young and Donna Tucker
Interiors courtesy of California Design Center, 14852 Beach Boulevard, Westminster, California

Contents

Introduction

Trip Around the World is a name often associated with quilts that have rows of squares forming their design. Since this is true of all the quilts we have included, we have chosen to label them all as *Trip Around the World* quilts. Each quilt pattern does have its own name. Some are traditional, such as *Sunshine and Shadow* and *Streak of Lightning*; and some are new, such as *Navajo* and *Evening Shadows*. These new names were given only to differentiate between the designs and also be somewhat descriptive.

The traditional Amish *Sunshine and Shadow* and *Trip Around the World* quilts were quite different from the quilts we are presenting. The Amish are a religious sect with a strict code of behavior. Traditionally they only used solid colored fabrics. Wide borders with beautiful hand quilting were an integral part of every quilt.

We have adapted these quilts to fit today's lifestyles. We feel that it is a natural progression in quiltmaking to render a traditional design in a contemporary way. We use print fabrics in a planned arrangement. Our quilts are machine pieced and hand quilted.

Although all of these designs are exciting in themselves, the purpose of this book is to introduce a new approach in their construction. This method is a new, easier way to make these traditional designs.

We were introduced to Seminole Indian patchwork in 1972. We soon began to apply those techniques to allover designs instead of bands of patchwork. By referring to photographs of completed *Trip Around the World* quilts, we were able to divide the quilts into sections. By counting the total number of squares in each row of a section, we noticed a pattern. Each row had two more squares than the previous row. From this we were able to chart the designs and plan sewing layouts. From the beginning we have worked with rows of squares instead of cutting strips of fabric. We feel more accuracy is achieved this way.

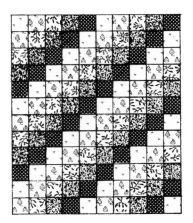

Trip Around the World was the first quilt we made with this method. However, we didn't realize that we should have figured the diagonal measurement of the squares. Since the diagonal measurement is larger, the quilt was huge!

We have been making these quilts (and teaching others to make them) since 1974. In that time we have changed and improved our techniques. One thing has remained the same: Quiltmakers welcome techniques that are efficient. This method involves the cutting and sewing of rows of squares instead of single squares. This is efficient use of both fabric and time.

How To Use This Book

The basic instructions for making the templates, marking and cutting the fabrics, and the sewing techniques apply to all the different quilts. Each of the quilts have their own specific instructions that apply to that pattern only. Read the basic instructions and then proceed to the quilt of your choice. However, it will help to at least read through and understand the *Sunshine and Shadow* directions before you begin *Evening Shadows*, *Navajo*, or *Many Trips Around the World*. They are variations of the *Sunshine and Shadow* design.

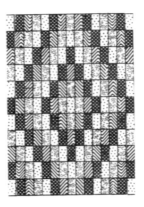

We have included charts for four sizes of quilts. They are approximately crib, twin, double-queen, and king bed sizes. Please measure your own bed to determine which chart to follow. We use the size of square that is in proportion to the size of the finished quilt. A crib sized quilt has 2-1/2" squares, a twin size has 3" squares, and the large queen and king sizes have 3-1/2" squares.

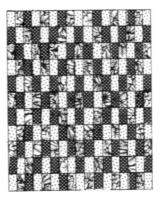

Directions are included for a number of smaller projects. Making one of these smaller projects, such as a pillow or wallhanging, is an excellent way to learn and understand the technique before starting a larger quilt. We have not shown every design in every size. Some designs will not be as effective in a smaller size. For instance, we do not show a crib sized *Navajo* quilt.

The most popular and versatile of these designs, *Trip Around the World* and *Sunshine and Shadow*, are shown in every size. They adapt well to different sizes and uses.

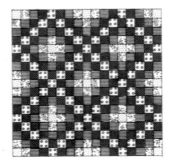

Yardage requirements for each quilt and project are listed below their sewing layout. Yardage requirements are figured for 42" wide fabric (45" wide fabric minus selvages.) Allow an extra quarter yard per yard on 36" - 42" wide fabrics. Other fabric amounts (backings, binding, ruffles) are listed under Yardage Charts. An easy method for figuring yardage is included in a handy chart form. In order to fully explore the design potential of these quilts, we have included directions for charting the quilts in any size, with any size of square.

Supplies

Posterboard   Posterboard is used for the templates. A firm plastic can also be used.

Ruler   Use a 12″ or 18″ ruler.

Graph paper   To chart and plan these quilts, use four-grids-to-the-inch graph paper.

Markers   A sharp No. 2 pencil will mark on most fabrics. Colored pencils or a dressmaker's chalk pencil may be necessary on very dark colors.

Scissors   Good, sharp scissors (shears) are a necessity. Many quilters have discovered Gingher brand scissors. They are excellent and will cut through several layers of fabric. Use paper scissors for the template.

Tape   This will be used on the fabric. The frosted Scotch tape will lift off easier than clear tape. The clear tape sometimes leaves a residue.

Pins   Extra-long glass headed dressmaker pins work best.

Thread   Use a good quality cotton covered polyester thread in a medium shade of the colors of the quilt.

Sewing Machine   This method was developed for machine piecing.

Spray starch   Use spray starch while pressing the fabrics. This will add body to all the fabrics and give stability to any lightweight or flimsy fabrics.

Thimble   Use a thimble when hand quilting.

Quilting thread   This is used for hand quilting (not in the sewing machine) and can also be used for basting.

Needles	Needles for hand quilting are called betweens. We use sizes 8, 9, and 10. Find the size that works best for you by purchasing a package of assorted sizes.
Batting	Polyester quilt batting is usually sold in packages by the quilt size. Bonded batting is sold by the yard and will require piecing.
Frames	A do-it-yourself frame can be made with four C-clamps and four boards (one-by-twos) from a hardware store. The boards should be longer than the quilt. These can be balanced on the backs of four chairs to make a handy frame for basting the quilt together. Once it is basted, it can be transferred to a smaller hoop for easier hand quilting.
Hoops	A large round or oval hoop is ideal for quilting. We use the standing oval hoop.

Fabrics/Color/Design

Fabrics

With the enormous amount of fabric available to the quiltmaker today, it's easy to feel overwhelmed. Here are some suggestions that should reduce some of the confusion you may feel when faced with selecting up to twelve different fabrics for one quilt!

You might begin by considering fiber content. 100% cotton and cotton/polyester blends are ideal for these quilts and are the most available. These woven fabrics should be a broadcloth weight. All fabrics should be spray starched after preshrinking. This will stabilize any fabrics that are lighter weight. A very loose weave fabric will fray and should be avoided.

Always try for an interesting mixture of prints. Instead of all small florals use dots, stripes, and geometric designs. Stripes should be narrow enough to show the whole pattern in every square. The quilts in color plates 16 and 18 both utilize stripes effectively. Even if all the prints are florals, look for ones with different amounts of background. Remember that every fabric does not have to be pretty or have a definite design. Prints that appear to be a solid color from a distance can be used to emphasize the other fabrics.

We look for prints with allover designs. A fabric with a large bouquet with lots of background showing will look like two different fabrics when cut. This could interfere with the design of the quilt. An exception to this is one of the fabrics in the quilt on the cover. The white-on-beige pin dot fabric had a tiny feather about every nine inches. This doesn't interfere with the design; instead, it adds a touch of whimsey to the quilt.

Vary the size of the figure in the print. Sometimes a large print will add just the right amount of pizzazz. It is the large paisley print that adds spice to the *Navajo* quilt in plate 20. Using large prints in quilts is not new. One only needs to look at quilts made in the 19th century to realize this. Sometimes we become so accustomed to seeing quilts with all tiny calicos, that we forget we can use anything else. Refer to the quilt in plate 6 to see the result of using just one large print. Two large prints next to each other will create a lacy effect, as in the quilt in plate 27. Solid color fabrics can be used but will not blend as well or be as interesting as prints.

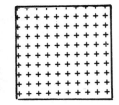

A mixture of prints

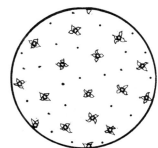

Different amounts of background

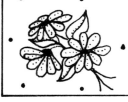

Too much background

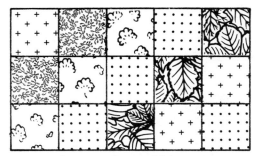

Large prints add interest

Color

The color of your fabric is probably more important to you than its fiber content, weave or print. The color information that we present here is meant to increase your awareness of color. We certainly do not intend for you to plan a color scheme with a color wheel and then set out to find corresponding fabrics. In fact, most of us have things like wallpaper patterns and carpet colors spinning around in our heads instead of terms like triad and split-complementary! We realize that reaction to color is very personal, however here are some things to consider when choosing colors.

There is pure color, or hue.
Separate from these are black and white.
Add white to a color to create tint.
Add black to a color to create shade.
Add white and black to a color to create tone.
White and black together create gray.
Intensity is the strength of a color.
Value is the lightness or darkness of a color.

The color circle contains the primary colors of red, blue, and yellow; the secondary colors of violet, green, and orange; and the intermediate colors of red-violet, blue-violet, blue-green, yellow-green, yellow-orange, and red-orange. Possible color harmonies using the color wheel include the following:

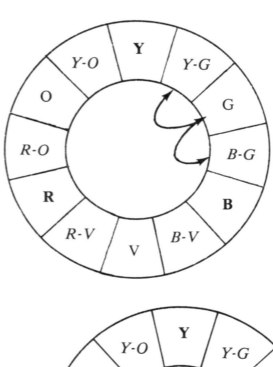

Analogous	These are colors that are next to each other on the color circle. Good color schemes are achieved when the key hue is a primary or secondary. The quilt in plate 35 used the analogous scheme of green with yellow-green and blue-green.

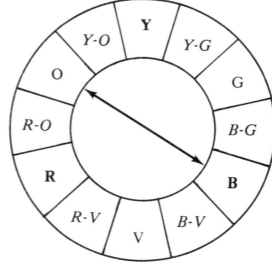

Complements	These are colors opposite each other on the circle. Colors opposite tend to heighten the intensity of each other. Combinations of a primary with a secondary are very basic and direct. Examples of these are the red and green in plates 45 and 47, and the orange and blue in plates 1 and 28. Combinations of intermediates are more sophisticated. An example of this is the red-violet and yellow-green in plate 25.

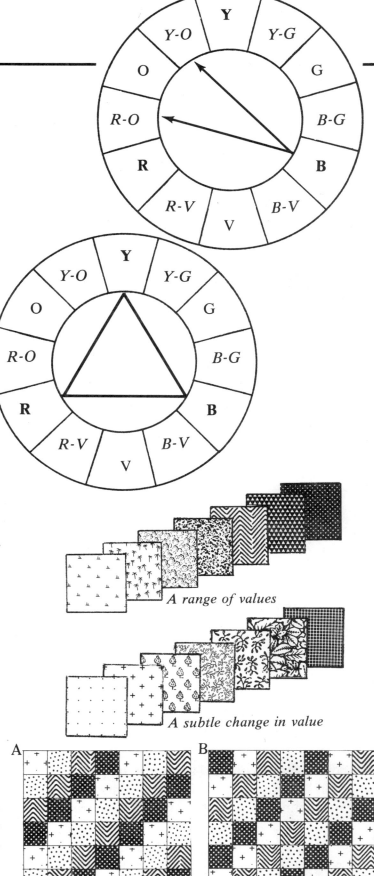

Split-Complements With this arrangement a color is combined with the two colors that are on either side of the color on the exact opposite. There are more possible combinations with split-complements than with complements alone.

Triads This is an equal triangle on the color circle. Yellow, blue, and red is the simplest and most direct. Even this combination can look more interesting by using unequal amounts of each color. The quilt in plate 2 has five blue fabrics, and three red fabrics. The prints contain touches of yellow.

Analogous colors tend to have an emotional quality since they can be warm (red, orange, yellow) or cool (green, blue, violet). Opposite colors have a visual quality, not only because they heighten the intensity of each other, but because they usually set a warm color against a cool one.

Most people instinctively choose good color arrangements, whether analogous, complementary, etc. What we want to do is increase your awareness of *value*. Again, value is the lightness or darkness of a color. A range of values is very important when working with one color or closely related colors. One example would be the monochromatic (one color) arrangement in plate 37. It shows different values of blue. We strive for a subtle change in value. This is what we call blending the fabrics. The quilt in plate 6 is a good example of this.

Something else that we feel is important is the sequence of the different values. Looking at these two examples, most people would choose illustration A as the most pleasing. Illustration B tends to look choppy. This would give a quilt a checkerboard look.

A range of values

A subtle change in value

A

B

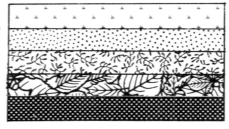

Light to dark fabric arrangement

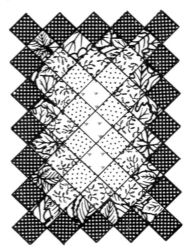

We think that the colors are more effective when the values of the fabrics are arranged light to dark. In most cases, we recommend a light to dark fabric arrangement rather than one that is dark to light. This is because of the visual "weight" of color. Darker colors appear "heavier" than light ones. Using the light to dark arrangement in the *Trip Around the World* quilt places the darkest color on the outer edges of the quilt. Viewing the bed from the side, the "heaviest" color is on the bottom.

Because the sequence of fabrics is repeated in these quilts, the darkest will be next to the lightest. This will cause the dark fabric to appear darker, and the light fabric appear lighter.

You can use light to dark arrangements within each color in the quilt. The *Trip Around the World* quilt in plate 30 has different values of rust and different values of brown. They are arranged light to dark within each color. The quilt in plate 40 has light to dark yellow and light to dark green.

Light to dark within each color

When combining several colors for these quilts remember that hues that are normally light in value when pure (such as orange, yellow-orange, yellow, yellow-green, green) look best as tints. Hues that are normally dark in tone (such as red, red-violet, violet, blue-violet, blue) look best as shades. The best example of this is the quilt in plate 4. There are tints of yellow combined with shades of blue.

Contrast effects between colors are most noticeable when the colors are closer in value. The oranges and blues in the *Streak of Lightning* quilt in plate 1 are fairly close in value. This increases the contrast in color, which also emphasizes the design. Another example is the Christmas tablecloth in plate 45. The values of red and green contrast better than a lighter value of red (pink) would with the same green.

We try to never use equal amounts of the different colors in our quilts. The quilt in plate 30 has eight fabrics, five brown and three rust. This adds up to approximately 65% brown and 35% rust.

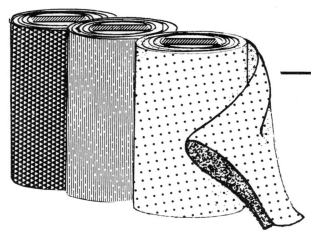

Now, amid all this information, a few simple words of advice: Whether you are in a yardage shop or sorting through your fabric collection at home, *begin with one fabric.*

Then select others that are lighter and darker.
Arrange the order of the fabrics from light to dark.
Select fabrics in a second or third color (analogous, complementary, etc.)
Rearrange the order of the fabrics if necessary.
Arrange the fabrics displaying the same amount of each.
Always look at them from a distance also.

Once the fabrics and arrangement are chosen, cut and tape a small swatch of each to a piece of paper. Record your arrangement by numbering the fabrics.

Displaying the same amount of each fabric

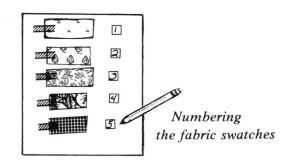

Numbering the fabric swatches

Design

The *Trip Around the World* quilt and its variations, are basically one-patch patterns. There is only one geometric shape in the quilt; a square or a rectangle. The fabric placement forms the design. These illustrations demonstrate how the different designs are formed by altering the placement of the fabrics.

In these illustrations the fabrics are used in the same sequence. This is true of most of the quilts in this book. Repeating the fabrics in the same sequence is effective, orderly, and emphasizes the design. Notice how much more effective the design is when the fabrics are repeated in sequence. Using the same sequence of fabrics also simplifies every step of making the quilt. The sequence can be repeated in reverse as a variation.

Sunshine and Shadow

Streak of Lightning

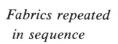

Fabrics repeated in sequence

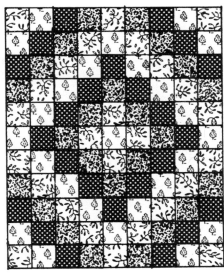

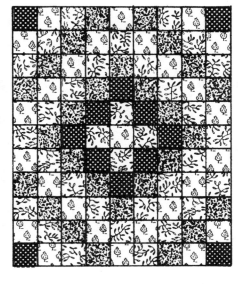

Fabrics randomly placed

7

Making the Templates

The quilts in this book are comprised of squares or rectangles. However, the squares and rectangles are not individually cut. They are marked, cut, and sewn as rows of squares or rows of rectangles.

There are several ways to mark a large piece of fabric into rows of squares. Originally, we did it with a single square template. The rows were sometimes wobbly. Then we tried marking them with a plastic ruler. This method was fine with 4″ squares, but when the square was 2-1/4″, more time was spent adding and figuring than marking.

Finally, we devised a multiple template. We've found this to be the easiest and most accurate. A multiple template is simply a cardboard row of squares with notches or slots between the squares. Marking around a multiple template will result in perfect squares in a straight line.

To make a multiple template, trace a single square between two parallel lines or along the edge of a piece of posterboard. Angle the sharpened pencil, drawing close to the square. Tracing around a template enlarges the pattern the width of a pencil line. The lines on the fabric from a multiple template will be a pencil line larger on the horizontal edges. Allowing a pencil line of space between the squares on the template will keep them square on the fabric.

We've already allowed this space between the squares in the templates provided in the back of the book. These templates are ready to cut out and use. Cut the slots out carefully, wide enough for a pencil point. Lift up the flap and remove. You may want to use these templates as master patterns to make more templates. Always trace around patterns carefully, angling the pencil to prevent distortion. A firm plastic will make a durable template. Just place the plastic over the template and trace them.

Sandpaper can be glued on the back of the templates to reduce slippage. Even pieces of two-sided tape, or rolled-up scotch tape, will help the template "grab" the fabric.

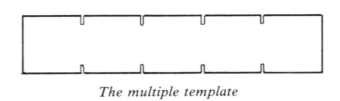

The multiple template

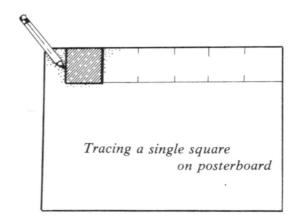

Tracing a single square on posterboard

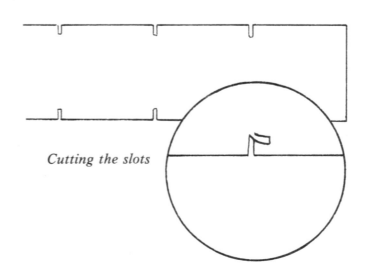

Cutting the slots

Marking and Cutting the Fabrics

Marking

The working area should accommodate the full width of the fabric. Choose the lightest colored fabric or the least busy print to mark first. Place it on top of another fabric for stability.

Square off the fabric by folding down the cut edge and creasing it. You could also use an L-square ruler or draftmans' triangle to draw a line that is perpendicular to the selvage. Tearing a fabric does not necessarily square it.

Starting 1/2″ from the right hand selvage, place the template on the creased or drawn line. Mark on the wrong side of the fabric keeping the pencil close to the template. Trace around the long edges of the template, then mark in the slots. Always mark in the center of the slots. Don't trace the left hand end of the template. Overlap the marked squares, matching the slots, and continue marking. Continue overlapping until the row is completed.

Mark the next row directly under the first. The rows will have a common line between them. Mark the number of rows needed. We will always list the number of rows to mark instead of the number of squares. However, if your fabric is less than 42″ wide each row will be short one square. Mark an extra row to make up for this.

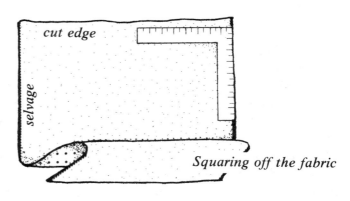

Squaring off the fabric

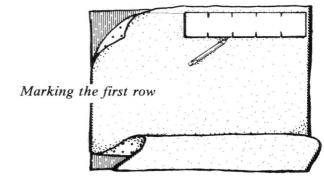

Marking the first row

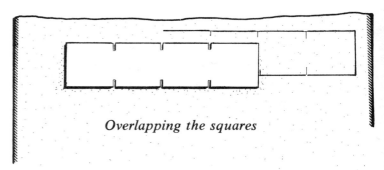

Overlapping the squares

The width of the fabric should yield:

Number of squares	Size of square
19	2-1/4″ cut/1-3/4″ sewn
17	2-1/2″ cut/2″ sewn
14	3″ cut/2-1/2″ sewn
12	3-1/2″ cut/3″ sewn
10	4″ cut/3-1/2″ sewn
17	2-1/2″ x 4-1/2″ cut/ 2″ x 4″ sewn (rectangle)

Yardage requirements have been figured for 42″ wide fabric (44″—45″ wide fabric minus sevages.) Allow an extra quarter yard per yard on 36″ to 42″ wide fabrics.

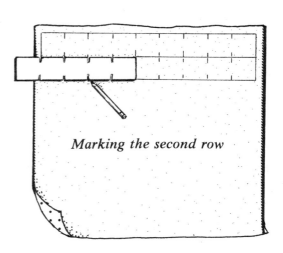

Marking the second row

Cutting

Several layers of fabrics can be cut together if your scissors will cut them accurately. We have cut eight layers with Gingher brand scissors. Only stack as many layers as you can comfortably cut.

Stack the fabrics with their right hand selvages together. You'll notice immediately that all the cut edges are different. Some will angle up and some down. Most permanent press fabrics cannot be pulled straight. Line up the right hand selvages and have the cut edges as even as possible. The squares will be straight on the lengthwise grain of the fabric, which is more important than the crosswise grain. Lay the marked fabric on top so that the squares will be on all the fabrics.

Pin the layers together using 5 or 6 pins on each row. Cut through all the layers, keeping the scissors upright. Cut off the excess at the top and sides. Carefully cut on all the crosswise lines. Do not cut into squares. Leave the pins in place.

At this stage only the top layer is marked into squares. To transfer these marks, snip the marked slots. Snip through all the layers keeping the scissors straight and the snips 1/4″ deep. Snip one edge of the row then without lifting or moving it, snip the other edge. We usually do this from the other side of the table. These snips will indicate the outline of each square. This is all the marking that is necessary with this method. Be sure to cut off any incomplete squares caused by narrower fabrics.

After the rows have been cut and snipped, separate the layers and group by fabric. Loosely fold the rows accordian-style, or hang them over a chair. Place them in the chosen sequence.

The fabrics for the *Trip Around the World* and *Many Trips Around the World* quilts require different amounts of each fabric. The fabrics can still be marked and cut together. Layer the fabrics with the larger pieces on the bottom. Mark the required numbers of rows on the first fabric. Trim the excess from the top fabric, cutting on the marked line. Mark the next fabric, placing the template at the cut edge of the top fabric. Mark the additional rows that the next fabric requires. Continue marking the rest of the fabric, trimming the excess from each. Pin each fabric after marking. After all the fabrics are marked, cut and snip the rows.

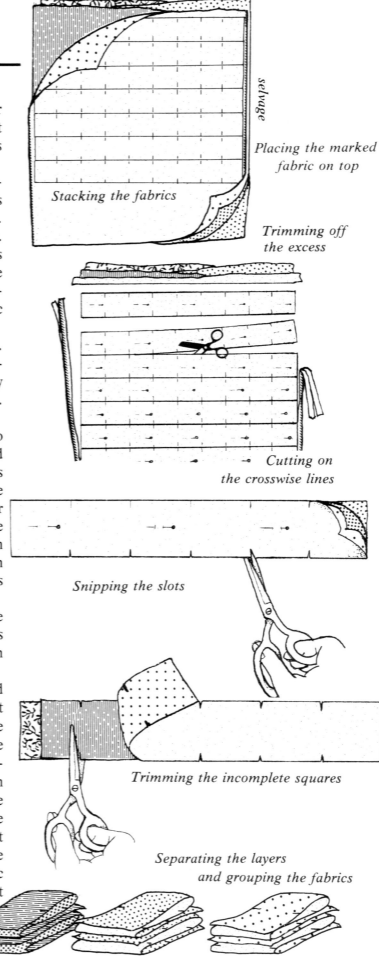

Placing the marked fabric on top

Stacking the fabrics

Trimming off the excess

Cutting on the crosswise lines

Snipping the slots

Trimming the incomplete squares

Separating the layers and grouping the fabrics

Following The Layout

You have probably noticed the charts that we use for these quilts. By sewing these rows of squares into a staggered arrangement, then cutting and resewing, the designs are formed. These arrangements are actually sewing layouts. Here is a basic description of the rows being arranged into a sewing layout. Each quilt pattern will have its own specific instructions.

Each row in the layout is usually increasing or decreasing. For example, in the *Sunshine and Shadow* layout, the first row is one square. The next row has three squares, and the next has five. You may be thinking it will be difficult to quickly count five squares on the fabric since the squares are only defined by little snips. We do mark the number of squares in each row of the layout but you don't need to count them. Simply follow the layout, increasing or decreasing each row.

Cut a single square from a row of squares. Place a row of the next fabric next to it. Cut the row so there is one square extending on each side. Continue in this manner, using the fabrics in sequence. Each row increases one square on each side, according to the sewing layout. Depending on the quilt size, there may be some rows that are the same size. Then the rows will begin to decrease, beginning with one square in the center, and then one square on each side. The rows will correspond to the sewing layout.

When cutting squares from the rows, cut straight from snip to snip. The scissor blade will reach from snip to snip on the smaller squares. With larger squares (3″, 3-1/2″), fold the row at the snips and cut.

Some rows in the layout require more squares than the width of the fabric will yield. To continue a row, place the ends together and tape. Do not overlap or sew them together, simply line them up and use tape to connect them for sewing. Some of the quilts have a row of single squares. Cut these squares last, in order to use the full rows for the longer rows in the layout. Stack these in order and pin.

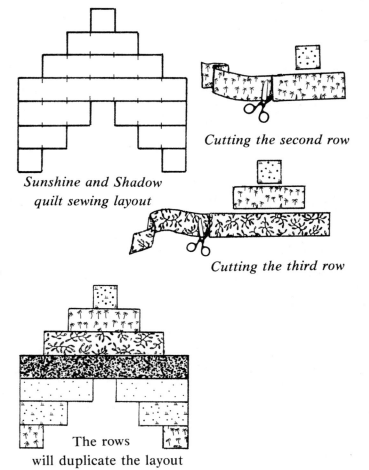

Sunshine and Shadow quilt sewing layout

Cutting the second row

Cutting the third row

The rows will duplicate the layout

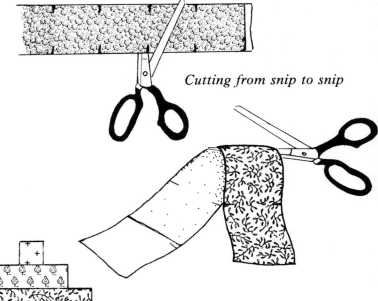

Cutting from snip to snip

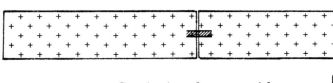

Continuing the rows with tape

The smaller projects can be arranged flat like the sewing layout. Laying out the quilts flat would require too much space. Follow the layout, but stack the rows on top of each other instead of next to each other. Pin at regular intervals.

In order to completely lay these out and still be able to transport them to another area for sewing, we use a handy aid. We stack the rows on a paper foundation. Use a narrow paper that comes on a roll. This could be paper towels, adding machine tape, or (dare we say it?) toilet tissue.

We use the paper as a foundation and as a cover for the rows. They can then be rolled up and unrolled without disturbing their order.

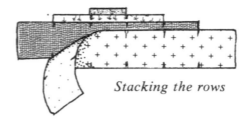

Stacking the rows

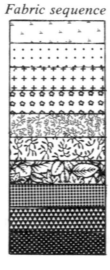
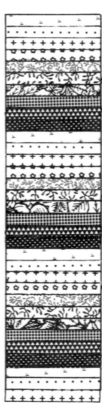
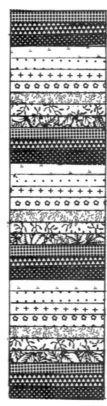

Repeating the fabrics in sequence

Fabric sequence *beginning with light fabrics* *beginning with dark fabrics*

The Fabric Placement

The number of different fabrics listed below each quilt layout is determined by the number of rows in that quilt. We try to use the number of fabrics that can be repeated about the same number of times. The same amount of each fabric will then be used. (Fabrics can be purchased and the color arrangement decided later since they each require the same amount.) Example: The sewing layout has 29 rows. Seven fabrics can be used in sequence, then repeated three times. The first fabric will be repeated again. (1 - 7, 1 - 7, 1 - 7, 1 - 7, 1) If the quilt were made with ten fabrics, they would be used in sequence, then repeated twice. (1 - 10, 1 - 10, 1 - 9) If this same quilt were made with twelve fabrics, a different amount of each would be required. The fabrics would be used in sequence, then repeated once. Then only five fabrics would be repeated again.

If a quilt layout has 33 rows and you have ten fabrics, you have the option of using them two different ways. They can be placed 1 - 10, 1 - 10, 1 - 10, 1, 2, 3. If the fabrics are arranged light to dark, this quilt would have a light center area. The quilt can have a dark center by placing the fabrics 8, 9, 10, 1 - 10, 1 - 10, 1 - 10. The fabrics are always used in sequence but you don't always have to start with the beginning of the sequence.

For a reverse sequence, as in the *Trip Around the World* quilts in plates 31 and 40, the fabrics are used in sequence and then repeated in reverse.

We list the number of fabrics and the amounts needed. If you want to use a different number of fabrics than listed, yardages must be figured. To do this, add up the squares needed of each fabric and refer to the yardage charts for the yardage equivalents.

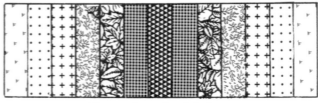

Repeating the fabric sequence in reverse

An asterisk (*) will be used to signify where to begin the fabric sequence. The *Sunshine and Shadow* and *Evening Shadows* quilts are made in three sections; two identical sections joined by a center row. The square in the middle of the center row is the exact center of the quilt. The fabric sequence begins there. The second fabric would be the first row in the layout. It would also be used for the two squares next to the middle square in the center row. Fabrics are used in the same sequence in the center row as well as in the rows of the sewing layout. *Trip Around the World* is also made in three sections. However, the same fabric is used for the center square as well as the first row in the layout.

Number your fabrics and write these numbers in the boxes on the rows. This makes the sewing layout easier to follow.

The fabric placement for the *Navajo* and *Many Trips Around the World* quilts is very important. Since these designs are formed with only a certain number of fabrics, the fabric numbers are printed in the boxes already.

Fabric sequence

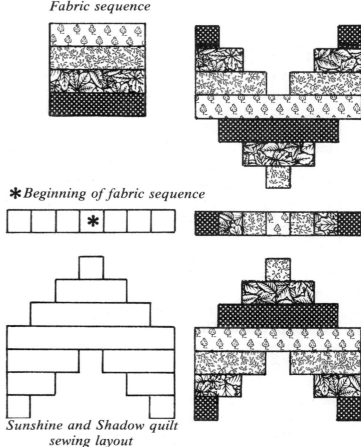

**Beginning of fabric sequence*

Sunshine and Shadow quilt sewing layout

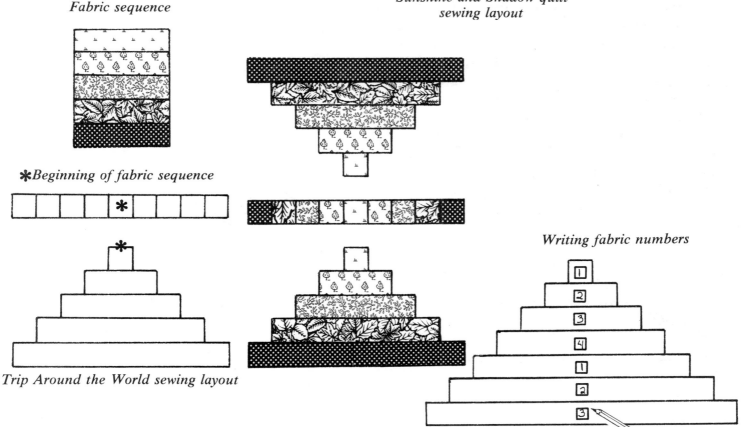

Fabric sequence

**Beginning of fabric sequence*

Trip Around the World sewing layout

Writing fabric numbers

Sewing Techniques

Sewing Techniques

The rows need to be cut and arranged according to the sewing layout before sewing. Whether you have arranged them flat, or stacked and rolled them, the rows should be on your right as you sit at the sewing machine. Even if you are left-handed, placing them on the right will be easier since each row is sewn to the right hand edge of the previous row. Completely unroll the rows on a table, a bed, or even the floor. Draping the rows over a chair or on your lap will disturb their order.

Begin at the top of the layout. This is always a single square. Place it right side up. Place the next row face down on top of it, matching the snips to the edges.

Sew with a 1/4 inch seam allowance, using 12 to 15 stitches per inch. The edge of the presser foot on some sewing machines may be slightly larger than 1/4 inch. Keep a consistent seam allowance even if it is not exactly 1/4 inch wide. Begin and end the stitching 1/4 inch beyond the snips instead of backstitching. Clip the threads as you sew.

Sew the row, then open it right side up. Place the next row face down on top and sew, matching the snips. These rows will eventually be cut apart, cutting from snip to snip. In order to cut them straight and have a straight seam, the snips must match.

It is much easier to match snips than marks. With marked squares, the rows must be turned over to see the marks. Snips can be matched from one side. The row can be slightly pulled and the snips will open slightly. They can then be matched exactly.

Always pin at the beginning and end of each row, and close to any taped edges. Pin elsewhere if needed.

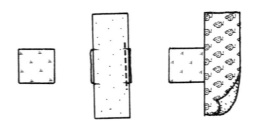

Sewing the rows

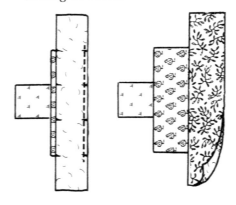

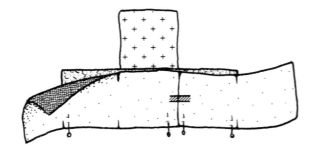

Pinning the rows

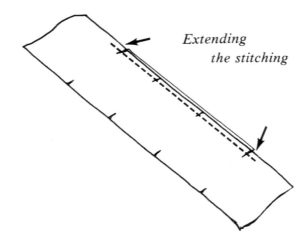

Extending the stitching

Now is a good time to acquaint yourself with the idiosyncrasies of your sewing machine. Most machines have a tendency to drag the top fabric and ease in the bottom fabric. This is caused by the pressure of the presser foot and the action of the feed mechanism. We've found that the layers will feed through more evenly if a finger is kept on the bottom fabric as well as the top fabric.

When sewing a heavy fabric to a lightweight or loose-weave fabric, the snips will look like they are not going to match. Hold firm on the heavy fabric and relax the pressure on the lightweight one and they will match.

If the snips are more than 1/4 inch apart don't try to force them to match. Instead, lay the template back on the rows to see which of the two squares is correct. Perhaps there was a fold in one of the fabrics during the cutting. This would result in a larger square when the fabric is smooth. Trim off any excess fabric or replace a too small square.

Continue to add the rows in this manner. Each successive row is placed on top of the previously sewn rows. The sewn rows will exactly duplicate the sewing layout.

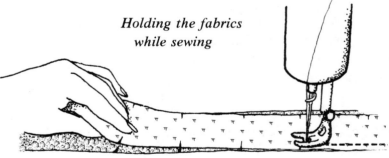

Holding the fabrics while sewing

Matching the snips

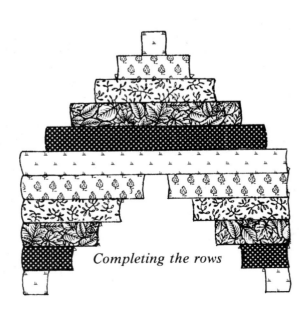

Completing the rows

Pressing

Press the sewn rows on the wrong side of the fabric. Remove any tape before pressing. The seam allowances should be pressed to one side. Alternate the direction of pressing. The first seam will be pressed up, the next seam pressed down, the next up, and the next down. After pressing the entire piece this way, turn it over and lightly press on the right side. This removes any folds that may have been caused by the pressing.

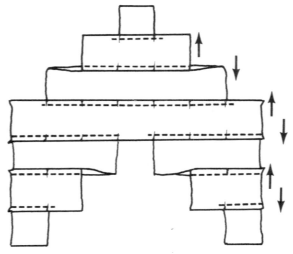

Alternate the direction of pressing

Cutting

Lay the piece on a large flat surface. These sewn rows will now be cut into rows of squares. The snips indicate the cutting line. This can be done without further marking with a good pair of scissors and a good eye. The scissors blade will reach from snip to snip in one stroke on the smaller sizes of squares. If you don't have confidence in your cutting ability or if you simply prefer having a line to follow, draw from snip to snip. Use the template or a ruler (not a yardstick) as a guide.

As each row is cut, place it face down on top of the previous row matching the top edges. We sometimes begin cutting on several rows. Then we slide the piece down to finish cutting. But as each row is completely cut, we immediately place it on the stack. The cut rows must stay in the same order.

When all the rows are cut and stacked, pin them together at the top with a large safety pin. As before, keep these rows on the right hand side of the sewing machine. Place them right side down on a chair or table, or on the side of the sewing machine as shown in plate 2.

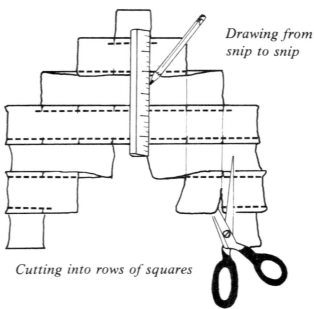

Drawing from snip to snip

Cutting into rows of squares

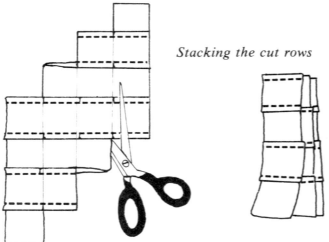

Stacking the cut rows

Pinning the cut rows

Sewing the Rows

Take the first row off the stack and turn it right side up. Place the next row face down on top of the first. It doesn't need to be turned over since it is already face down. Sew together, then open. Each successive row will be placed face down, sewn, and then opened. Sew with 1/4 inch seam allowances.

You will soon realize the reason for alternating the seams while pressing. Corners match better in machine piecing when the seams are facing opposite directions. All of these do this, allowing you to push them against each other. We have found that this results in a perfect match in almost every corner. We say "almost," because fabrics behave differently and some can be very uncooperative. Extensive pinning is not necessary when the seams alternate like this.

The presser foot on some machines may drag the seams away from each other when the top seam is away from the needle. Pin close to the seam to prevent this. Usually when the top seam is towards the needle the presser foot pushes them together, making a better match. Some machines can push the seam up and over the slight hump of the other seam. Prevent this by pinning the seam in place. We sometimes use a darning needle to guide the seam under the foot. When a corner doesn't match, don't resew the entire seam. Just remove the stitching and resew the area over the seams.

If the sewing is interrupted, always pin the remaining rows to the top of the last seam. This will prevent accidentally turning the whole piece upside down when the sewing is resumed.

Several of these quilts have a single row that is sewn separately from the other sections. They are single squares sewn into a row.

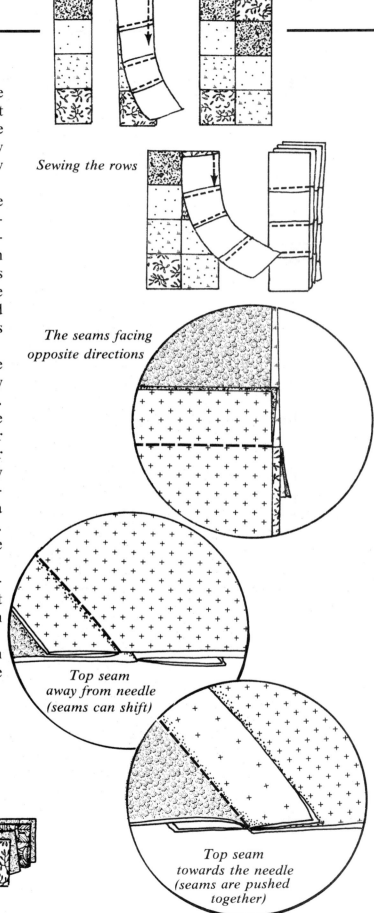

Sewing the rows

The seams facing opposite directions

Top seam away from needle (seams can shift)

Top seam towards the needle (seams are pushed together)

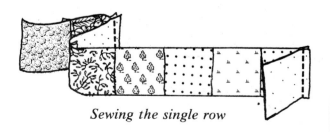

Sewing the single row

Pressing The Completed Sections

Press the completed sections and single row before joining. The seams of the two sections can be pressed the same direction. Press the seams of the single row the opposite direction. Another way is to press the seams in the sections in alternating directions. The seams in the single row should be pressed one direction and then the other. This will make the seams flip easily in either direction.

After the sections are sewn together, staystitch 1/4 inch on the outside edges. This will prevent the seams from being pulled apart at the edges during the finishing of the quilt.

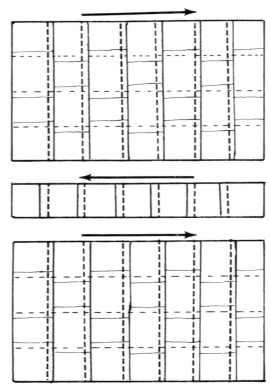

Pressing in opposite directions

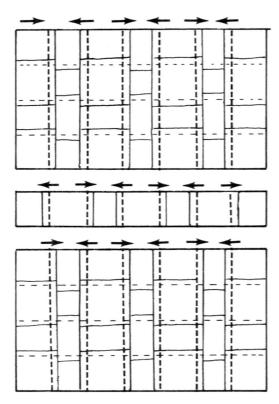

Pressing in alternating directions

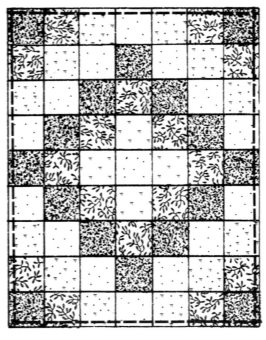

Staystitching the completed top

Streak of Lightning

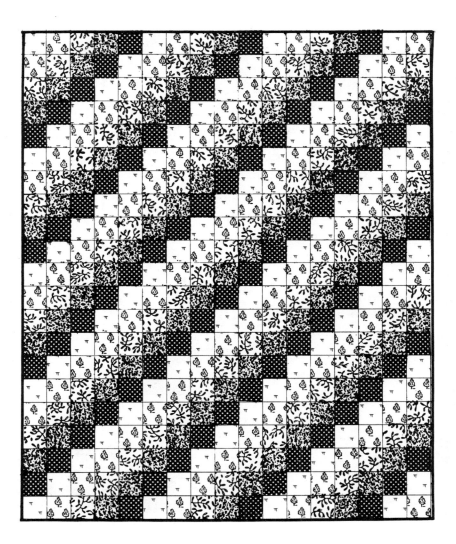

Streak of Lightning is a simple diagonal design. Using two colors will emphasize this design. If two fabrics that are very similar in color and value are placed next to each other in the quilt, it will give a zig-zag or lightning effect.

Color photographs of Streak of Lightning quilts are shown on page 25.

Streak of Lightning

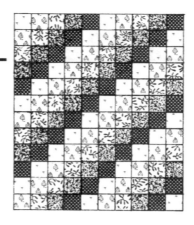

Follow the basic instructions for cutting and sewing the rows.

The *Streak of Lightning* quilt is made in one piece. The sewing layout is for the entire quilt.

Beginning with one square, each row increases one square on one side. This continues until the rows are the width of the quilt. Depending on the quilt, there may be some rows that are the same size.

Each row will then decrease by one square on the opposite side, ending with one square.

The diagonal design will go from the lower left to the upper right of the quilt if the fabrics are stacked face down. To reverse the design, follow the layout but stack the fabrics right side up.

The sewn rows of squares will duplicate the sewing layout. Be sure to press the seams in alternating directions. As the rows are cut apart, carefully place them face down on each other. They will then be in the correct order as they are lifted off the stack and sewn together.

*The sewn rows duplicate
the sewing layout*

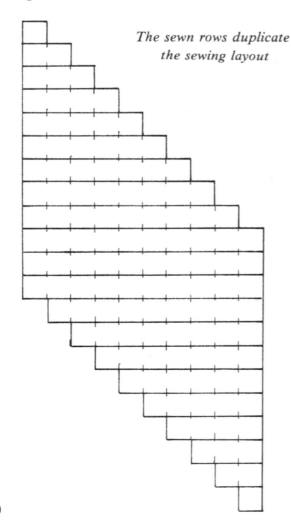

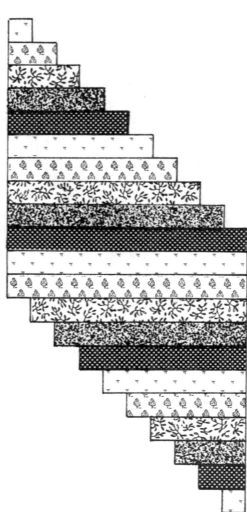

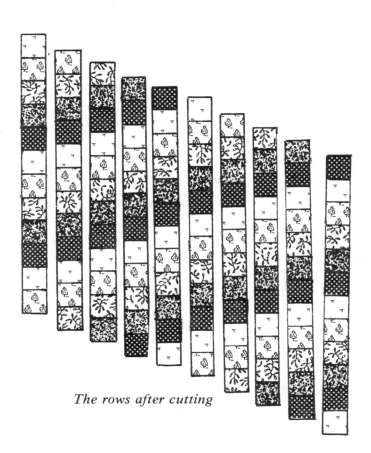

The rows after cutting

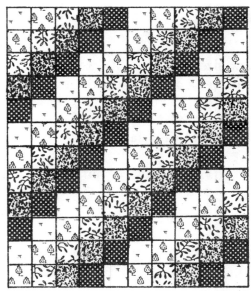

The rearranged rows now form the design

21

Streak of Lightning

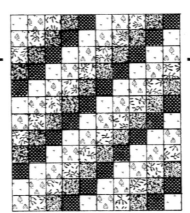

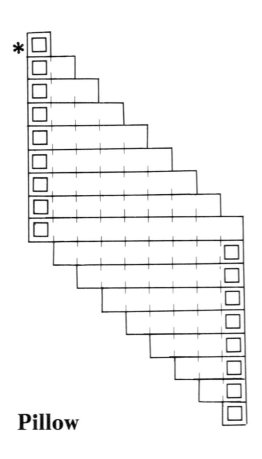

Pillow

Pillow size — 15-3/4" × 15-3/4"
Square — 1-3/4" (sewn)

Five fabrics — 1/8 yard each
Cut 1 row of each fabric

Total rows in sewing layout — 17

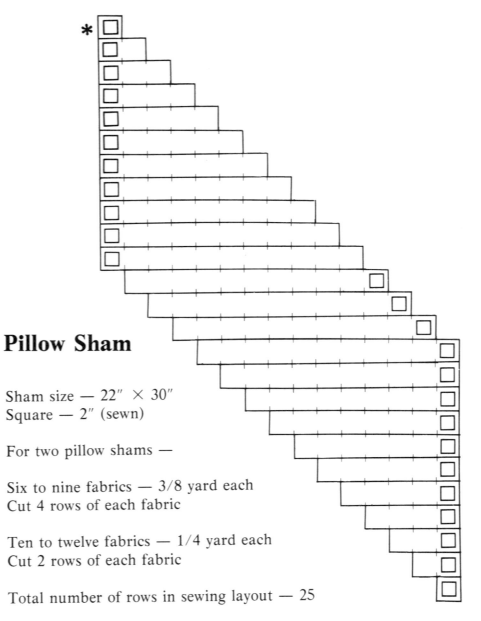

Pillow Sham

Sham size — 22" × 30"
Square — 2" (sewn)

For two pillow shams —

Six to nine fabrics — 3/8 yard each
Cut 4 rows of each fabric

Ten to twelve fabrics — 1/4 yard each
Cut 2 rows of each fabric

Total number of rows in sewing layout — 25

* Begin fabric sequence here.
☐ Write fabric number here.

Streak of Lightning

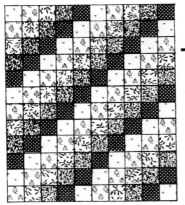

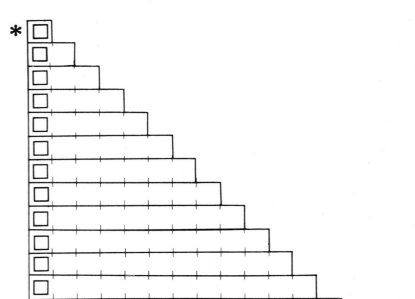

Quilt

Crib size — 42" × 52"
Square — 2-1/2" (sewn)

Seven fabrics — 1/2 yard each
Cut 4 rows of each fabric

Total rows in sewing layout — 37

* Begin fabric sequence here.
□ Write fabric number here.

Streak of Lightning

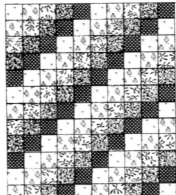

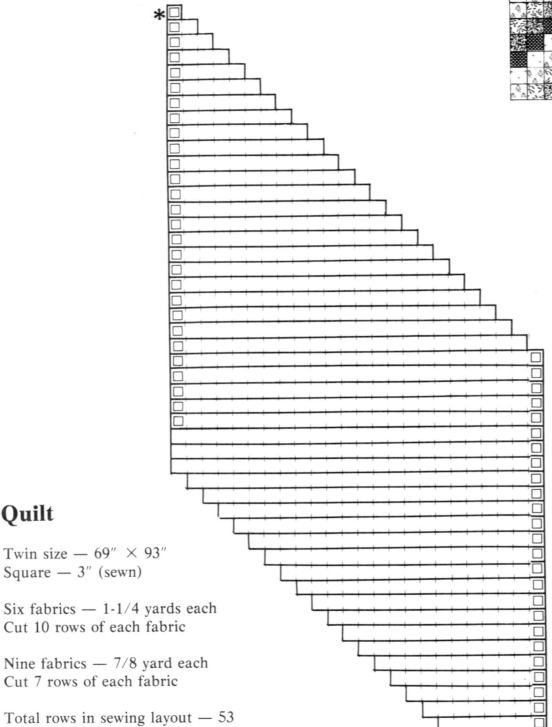

Quilt

Twin size — 69″ × 93″
Square — 3″ (sewn)

Six fabrics — 1-1/4 yards each
Cut 10 rows of each fabric

Nine fabrics — 7/8 yard each
Cut 7 rows of each fabric

Total rows in sewing layout — 53

✳ Begin fabric sequence here.
☐ Write fabric number here.

1 *Streak of Lightning* (70″ × 90″) by Blanche Young.

2 *Streak of Lightning* by the authors. This photograph demonstrates a phase of the construction.

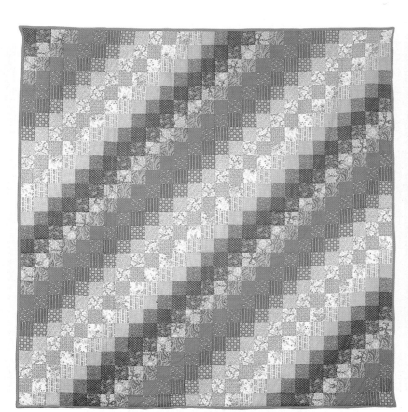

3 *Streak of Lightning* (94″ × 94″) by Beverly Cheryl Allen. This simple diagonal design can be very dramatic, as shown here.

4 *Streak of Lightning* (42″ × 50″) by the authors. The prairie points edging adds an extra touch to this baby quilt.

5 *Sunshine and Shadow* (88″ × 94″) by Blanche Young. (Quilt courtesy of Mr. and Mrs. James Bingham)

6 *Sunshine and Shadow* (88″ × 94″) by Blanche Young. This quilt top shows the effective use of a monochromatic color scheme.

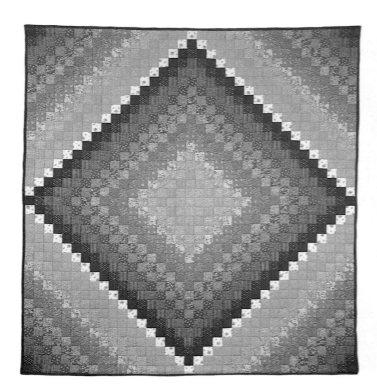

7 *Sunshine and Shadow* (105″ × 111″) Fabric arrangement by Blanche Young, pieced by Beverly Cheryl Allen, quilted by Coreen Kline.

8 *Sunshine and Shadow* (93″ × 99″) by Maridel Schrader. Note that these fabrics are repeated in the same sequence twice.

9 The very traditional design of *Sunshine and Shadow* is shown in a very contemporary setting.

10 *Sunshine and Shadow* (88″ × 94″) by Sharon Rangel. Fabrics were expertly combined in this quilt. (Also shown in Plate 9)

11 *Sunshine and Shadow* (88″ × 94″) by Blanche Young. Repeating the fabrics in the same sequence emphasizes the diagonal square design.

12 (above) *Sunshine and Shadow* (42″ × 52″) Pieced by the authors; quilted by Pat Perry. The quilting parallels the design of this crib sized quilt.

13 (right) Any baby would be delighted with a quilt like Heather's.

14 This *Sunshine and Shadow* quilt top is Blanche Young's answer to a friend's request for a purple quilt. It features an unusual array of prints as well as several shades of purple. (Quilt courtesy of Barbara Bates)

15 (above) This wallhanging by Helen Young features the colors and borders of a typically Amish *Sunshine and Shadow* quilt. The squares measure 1-1/2 inches. It has been mounted on stretcher bars for a modern look.

16 (right) April Chaney's beautiful *Sunshine and Shadow* has been carefully basted and is now ready for quilting.

17 (left) *Navajo* (90″ × 109″) by Angie Murray. This design is actually a variation of *Sunshine and Shadow*. This quilt features an uncommon mix of prints and dramatic use of color.

18 (below) *Navajo* (90″ × 101″) by Rea March.

19 (left) *Navajo* (106″ × 109″) by Nancy Hall. Nancy has increased the visual impact of this quilt by carefully blending the blue fabrics.

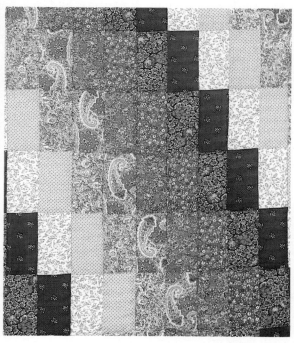

21 (above) Detail, *Navajo*. The very subtle color change in the fabrics and the use of a larger scale paisley print make this quilt an outstanding example of this design.

20 (above) *Navajo* (90″ × 109″) by Blanche Young.

22 (right) The bold design of this quilt makes it the focal point of any room.

31

23 The polished cotton fabrics contribute to the elegance of this *Sunshine and Shadow* tablecloth by Gail Giberson.

24 This *Sunshine and Shadow* tablecloth by Blanche Young adds charm to this casual setting.

Streak of Lightning

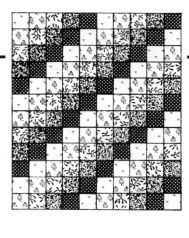

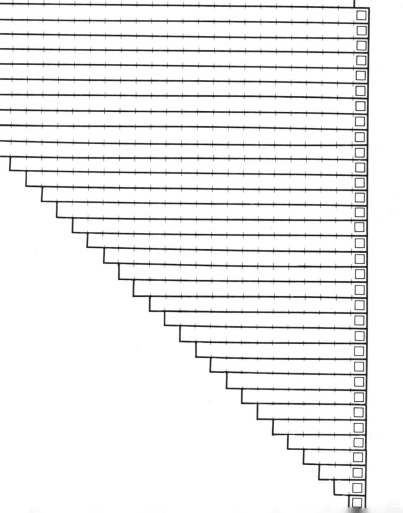

Quilt

Double/Queen size — 87″ × 99″
Square — 3″ (sewn)

Seven fabrics — 1-3/8 yards each
Cut 12 rows of each fabric

Ten fabrics — 1 yard each
Cut 8 rows of each fabric

Total rows in sewing layout — 61

✱ Begin fabric sequence here.
□ Write fabric number here.

33

Streak of Lightning

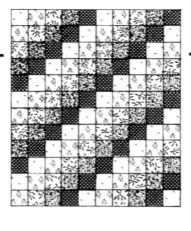

Quilt

King size — 101″ × 108″
Square — 3-1/2″ (sewn)

Eight fabrics — 1-5/8 yards each
Cut 12 rows of each fabric

Twelve fabrics — 1-1/8 yards each
Cut 8 rows of each fabric

Total rows in sewing layout — 59

✳ Begin fabric sequence here.
☐ Write fabric number here.

34

Sunshine and Shadow

This traditional design has continuing appeal to quilters. It is the most popular among our students. The straight edges lend themselves to borders. The design is striking when viewed flat, as in a wall-hanging. Its versatility is evident in the room setting in plate 41.

Color photographs of Sunshine and Shadow quilts are shown on pages 26 through 29.

Sunshine and Shadow

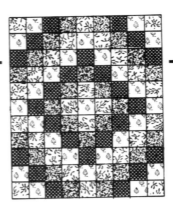

Follow the basic directions for cutting and sewing the rows.

The *Sunshine and Shadow* quilt is made in three sections; two identical sections and one single row of squares. Since the two sections are identical, the same sewing layout is followed for both. This quilt must have an odd number of squares for the design to be centered. The center square of the single row will be in the exact center of the quilt. Begin the fabric sequence there. The next fabric in the sequence is used for the first row of the layout. It would also be used next to the center square in the single row. The fabrics are used in sequence in the single row as well as in the sewing layout.

The sewing layout begins with one square. Each row increases one square on each side until the width of the quilt is reached. Depending on the quilt size, there may be some rows that are the same size.

The rows will then begin to decrease, starting with one square in the center. Each successive row will decrease one square on each side. The outer edges remain even.

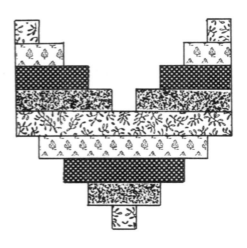

The sewn rows will duplicate the sewing layout. When they are cut and resewn, they will form the *Sunshine and Shadow* design.

Press in alternating directions before cutting. As the rows are cut apart, carefully place them face down on each other. They will then be in the correct order as they are lifted off the stack and sewn together.

Sew the separate squares together to form the single row. Join the three completed sections.

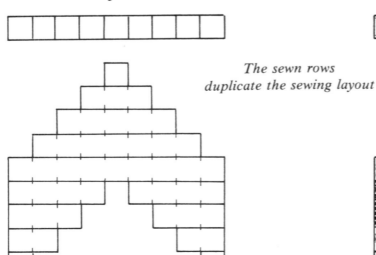

*The sewn rows
duplicate the sewing layout*

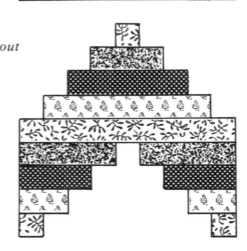

36

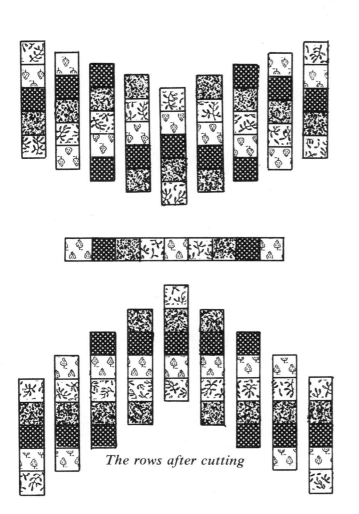

The rows after cutting

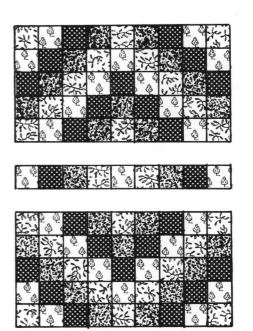

The rearranged rows now form the design

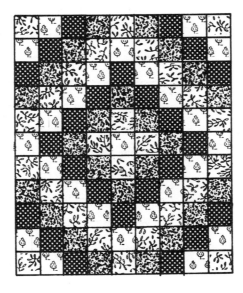

Sunshine and Shadow

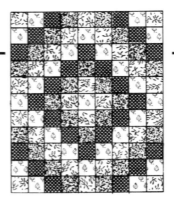

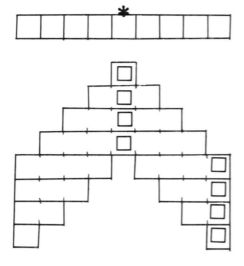

Pillow

Pillow size — 15-3/4″ × 15-3/4″
Square — 1-3/4″ (sewn)

Five fabrics — 1/8 yard each
Cut 1 row of each fabric

Total rows in sewing layout
(including single row) — 9

Quilt

Crib size — 42″ × 52″
Square — 2-1/2″ (sewn)

Seven fabrics — 1/2 yard each
Cut 4 rows of each fabric

Total rows in sewing layout
(including single row) — 19

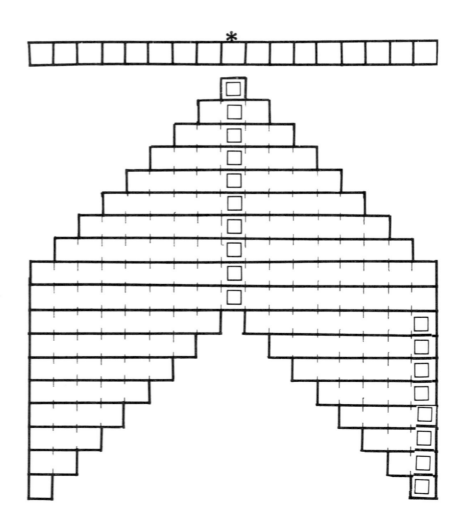

✱Begin fabric sequence here.
☐ Write fabric number here.

Sunshine and Shadow

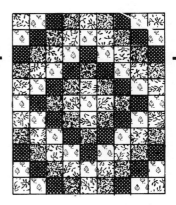

Pillow Sham

Sham size — 22" × 30"
Square — 2" (sewn)

For two shams —

Eight to ten fabrics — 3/8 yard each
Cut 3 rows of each fabric

Total rows in sewing layout
(including single row) — 13

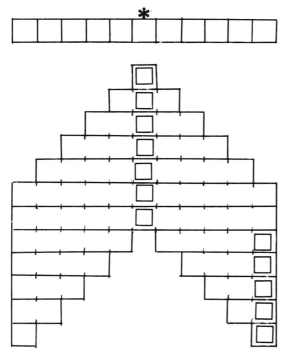

Tablecloth

Size 63" × 63"
Square — 3" (sewn)

Five fabrics — 7/8 yard each
Cut 8 rows of each fabric

Seven fabrics — 3/4 yard each
Cut 6 rows of each fabric

Tablecloth/Wallhanging

Size — 52" × 52"
Square — 2-1/2"

Five fabrics — 3/4 yard each
Cut 7 rows of each fabric

Seven fabrics — 5/8 yard each
Cut 5 rows of each fabric

Total rows in sewing layout
(including single row) — 21

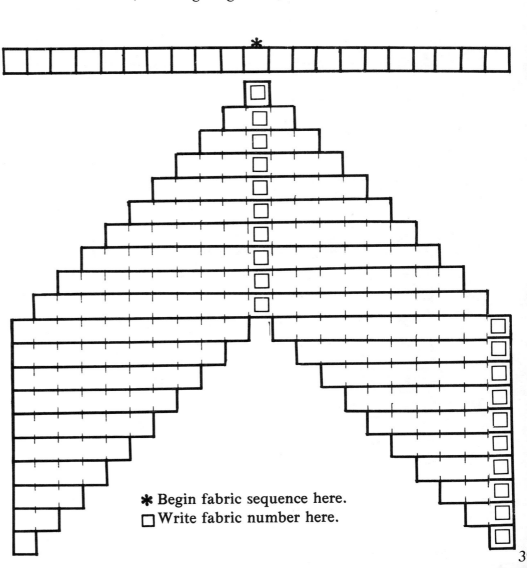

✳ Begin fabric sequence here.
☐ Write fabric number here.

Sunshine and Shadow

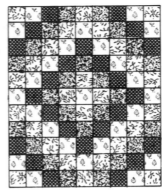

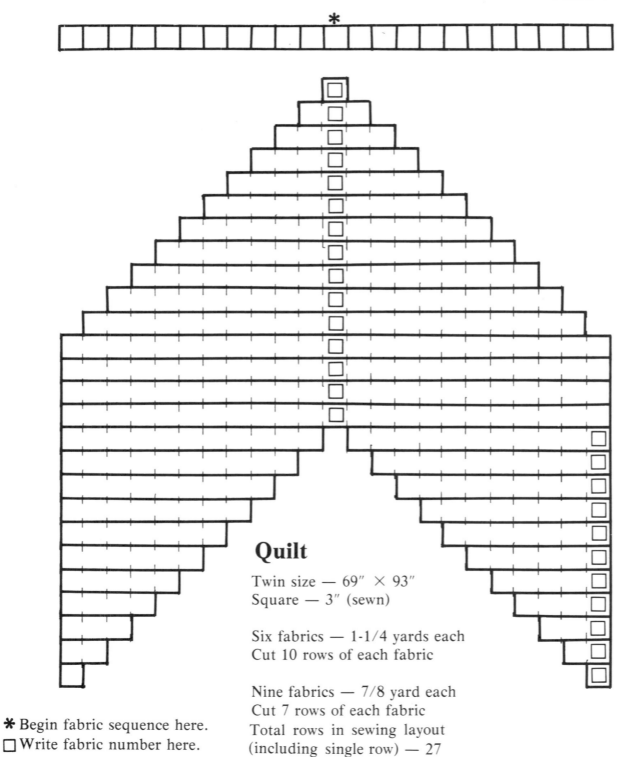

Quilt

Twin size — 69" × 93"
Square — 3" (sewn)

Six fabrics — 1-1/4 yards each
Cut 10 rows of each fabric

Nine fabrics — 7/8 yard each
Cut 7 rows of each fabric
Total rows in sewing layout
(including single row) — 27

✱ Begin fabric sequence here.
☐ Write fabric number here.

Sunshine and Shadow

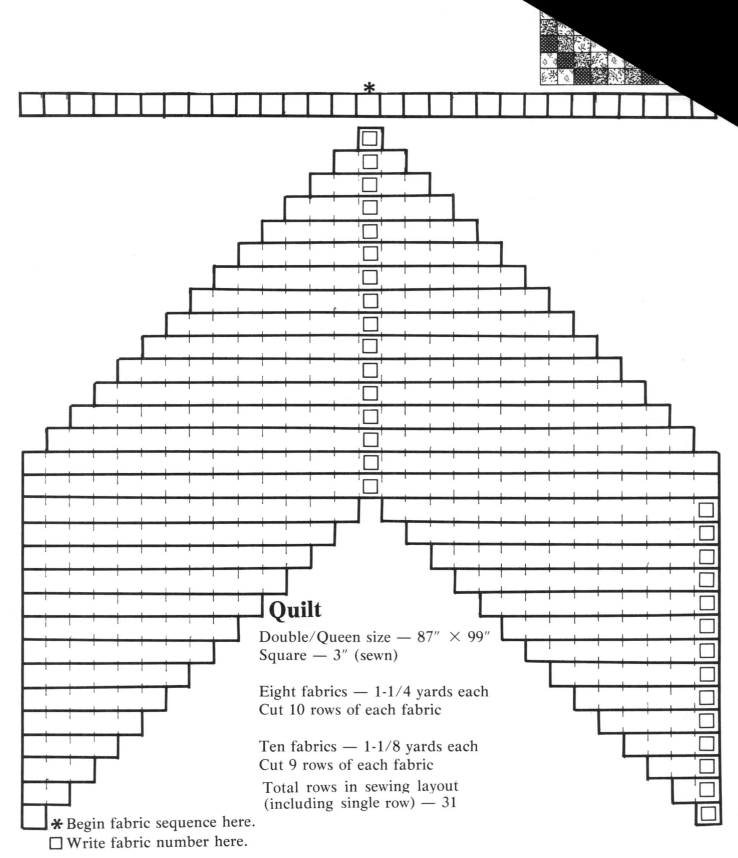

Quilt

Double/Queen size — 87" × 99"
Square — 3" (sewn)

Eight fabrics — 1-1/4 yards each
Cut 10 rows of each fabric

Ten fabrics — 1-1/8 yards each
Cut 9 rows of each fabric

Total rows in sewing layout
(including single row) — 31

✱ Begin fabric sequence here.
☐ Write fabric number here.

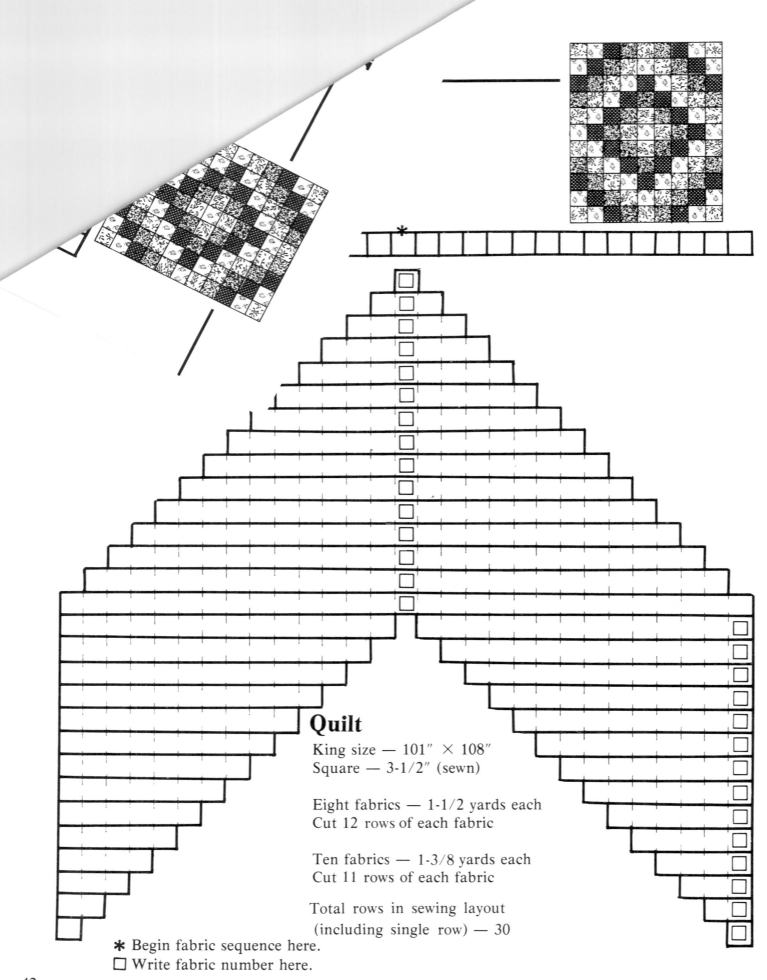

Quilt

King size — 101" × 108"
Square — 3-1/2" (sewn)

Eight fabrics — 1-1/2 yards each
Cut 12 rows of each fabric

Ten fabrics — 1-3/8 yards each
Cut 11 rows of each fabric

Total rows in sewing layout
(including single row) — 30

✱ Begin fabric sequence here.
☐ Write fabric number here.

Evening Shadows

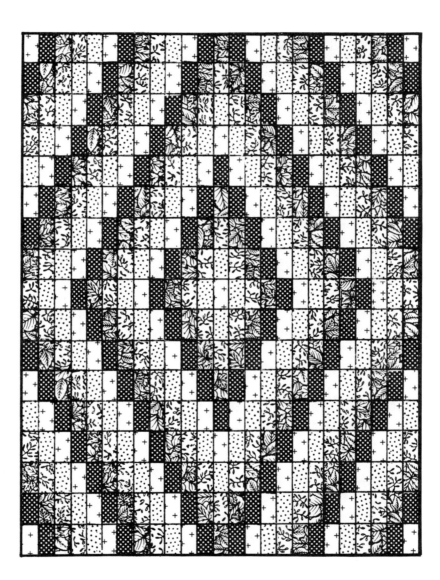

This design is an elongated *Sunshine and Shadow*. As in the evening when shadows lengthen, the squares have been lengthened into rectangles. The rectangles form a diamond, instead of a diagonal square design as in *Sunshine and Shadow*. Rectangles that are only slightly longer than their width are not as effective as longer rectangles. These rectangles are twice as long as their width.

Color photographs of an Evening Shadow quilt are shown on page 65.

Evening Shadows

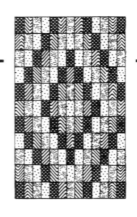

Follow the basic directions for cutting and sewing the rows.

The *Evening Shadows* quilt is made in three sections; two identical sections connected by a single row in the center. Since the two sections are identical, the same sewing layout is followed. The fabric sequence begins at the center rectangle of the single row. The next fabric would be used next to the center and for the first row of the layout. Fabrics are used in sequence in both the single row and in the sewing layout.

The sewing layout begins with one rectangle. Each row increases one rectangle on each side. According to the sewing layout, they will also begin to decrease from the center. Beginning with one rectangle in the center, each row will decrease one rectangle on the inside edge. Some of the rows will contain the same number of rectangles. As the layout indicates, the rows continue to decrease. Since there is not a row that extends the full width of the quilt, it is very important to stack the rows on a paper foundation.

The sewn rows of rectangles will duplicate the sewing layout. When they are cut and resewn, they will form the *Evening Shadows* design. Press the seams in alternate directions before cutting. Carefully place the cut rows face down on each other. Sew them together in the correct order, forming the top and bottom sections of the quilt. There will be twice as many vertical seams as horizontal seams.

Sew the separate rectangles together to form the single row. Join the three completed sections.

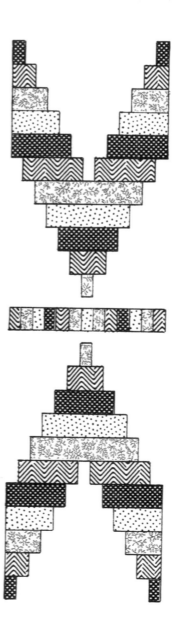

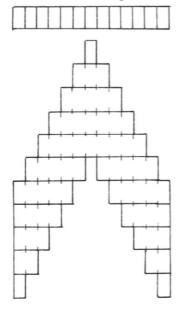

The sewn rows duplicate the sewing layout

44

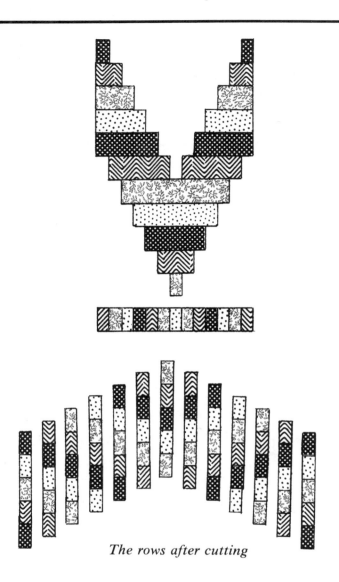

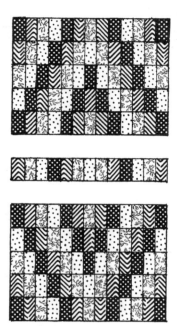

The rearranged rows now form the design

The rows after cutting

Evening Shadows

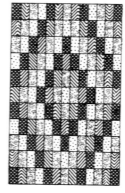

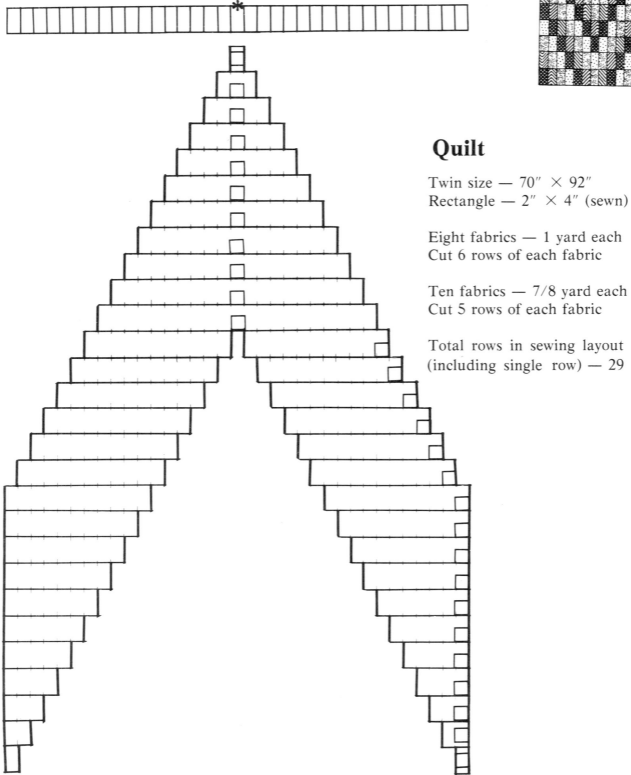

Quilt

Twin size — 70" × 92"
Rectangle — 2" × 4" (sewn)

Eight fabrics — 1 yard each
Cut 6 rows of each fabric

Ten fabrics — 7/8 yard each
Cut 5 rows of each fabric

Total rows in sewing layout
(including single row) — 29

*Begin fabric sequence here.
☐ Write fabric number here.

Evening Shadows

Quilt

Double/Queen size — 86″ × 100″
Rectangle — 2″ × 4″ (sewn)

Eight fabrics — 1-1/4″ yards each
Cut 8 rows of each fabric

Eleven fabrics — 1 yard each
Cut 6 rows of each fabric

Total rows in sewing layout
(including single row) — 34

*Begin fabric sequence here.
☐ Write fabric number here.

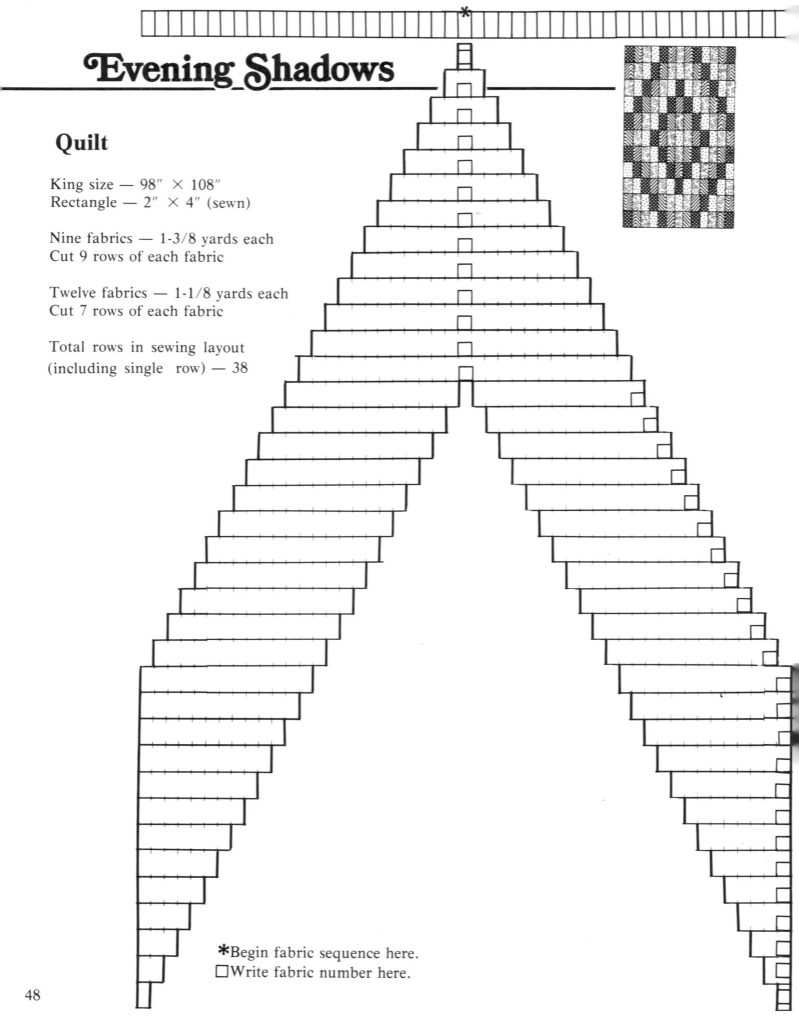

Evening Shadows

Quilt

King size — 98" × 108"
Rectangle — 2" × 4" (sewn)

Nine fabrics — 1-3/8 yards each
Cut 9 rows of each fabric

Twelve fabrics — 1-1/8 yards each
Cut 7 rows of each fabric

Total rows in sewing layout
(including single row) — 38

*Begin fabric sequence here.
□ Write fabric number here.

48

The *Navajo* quilt, named for its resemblance to a Navajo Indian rug, is another variation of *Sunshine and Shadow*. The fabrics form a diamond in the center and half-diamonds on the sides. We try to use one very dark fabric to outline the design. A specific number of fabrics is required to form this design. The fabrics are used in sequence, but their placement is very important. The correct fabric placement is printed in the boxes on the rows.

Color photographs of Navajo quilts are shown on pages 30 and 31.

Navajo

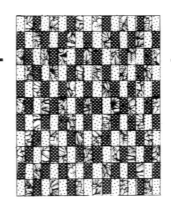

Follow the basic directions for cutting and sewing the rows.

The *Navajo* quilt is made in three sections; two identical sections connected by a single row in the center. Since the two sections are the same, the same layout is followed.

The sewing layout begins with three rectangles. Each row in the center increases by one rectangle on each end, the side rows increase by one rectangle on one end. Each row continues to increase as indicated on the layout. Depending on the quilt size, there may be some rows the same size. Beginning with one rectangle in the center and one on each end, the rows will decrease in size.

The sewn rows of rectangles will duplicate the sewing layout. When they are cut and resewn they will form the *Navajo* design. Press the seams in alternate directions before cutting. Carefully place the cut rows face down on each other. Sew them together in the correct order, forming the top and bottom sections of the quilt. There will be twice as many vertical seams as horizontal seams.

Sew the separate rectangles together to form the single row. Follow the fabric numbers carefully, since the fabrics are repeated in reverse. Join the three completed sections.

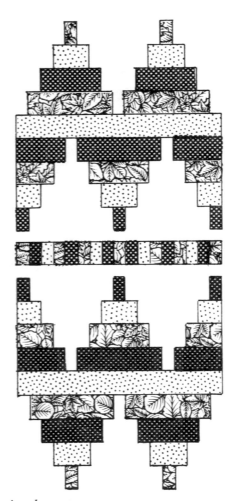

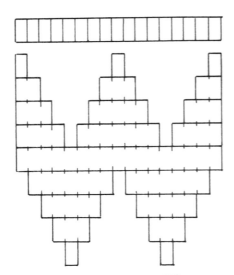

The sewn rows duplicate the sewing layout

50

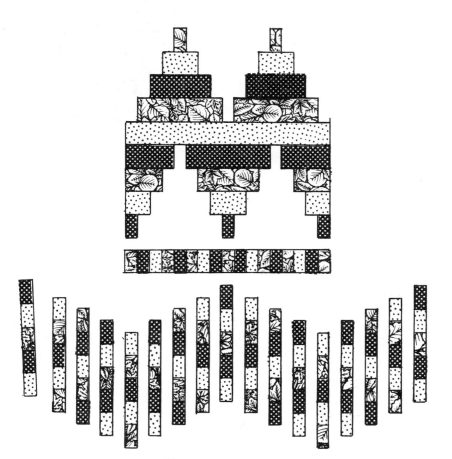

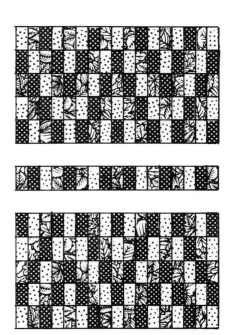

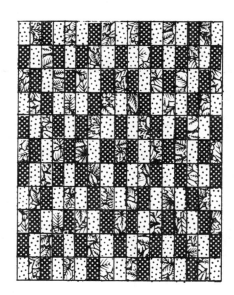

The rows after cutting

The rearranged rows now form the design

Navajo

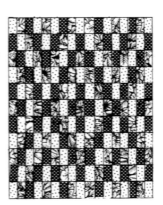

Quilt

Twin size — 74" × 92"
Rectangle — 2" × 4"

Seven fabrics — 1-1/4" yards each
Cut 8 rows of each fabric

Total rows in sewing layout
(including single row) — 23

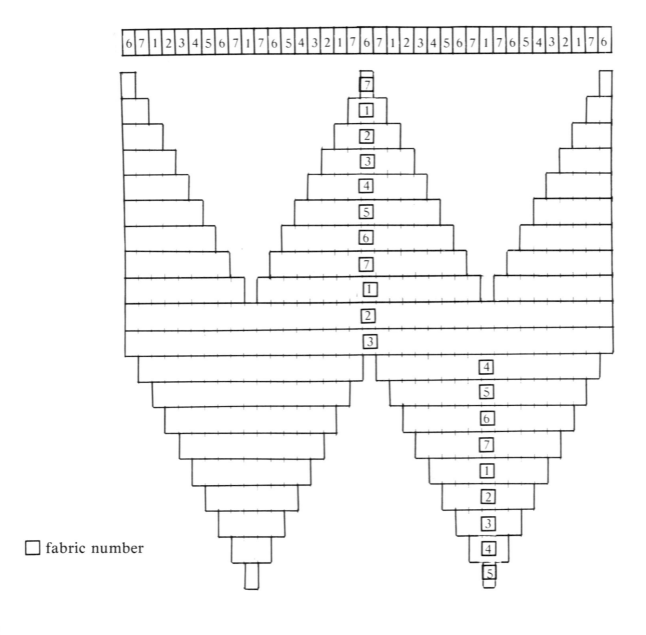

| 6 | 7 | 1 | 2 | 3 | 4 | 5 | 6 | 7 | 1 | 7 | 6 | 5 | 4 | 3 | 2 | 1 | 7 | 6 | 7 | 1 | 2 | 3 | 4 | 5 | 6 | 7 | 1 | 7 | 6 | 5 | 4 | 3 | 2 | 1 | 7 | 6 |

☐ fabric number

Navajo

Quilt

Double/Queen size — 90″ × 100″
Rectangle — 2″ × 4″

Eight fabrics — 1-3/8 yards each
Cut 9 rows of each fabric

Total rows in sewing layout (including single row) — 24

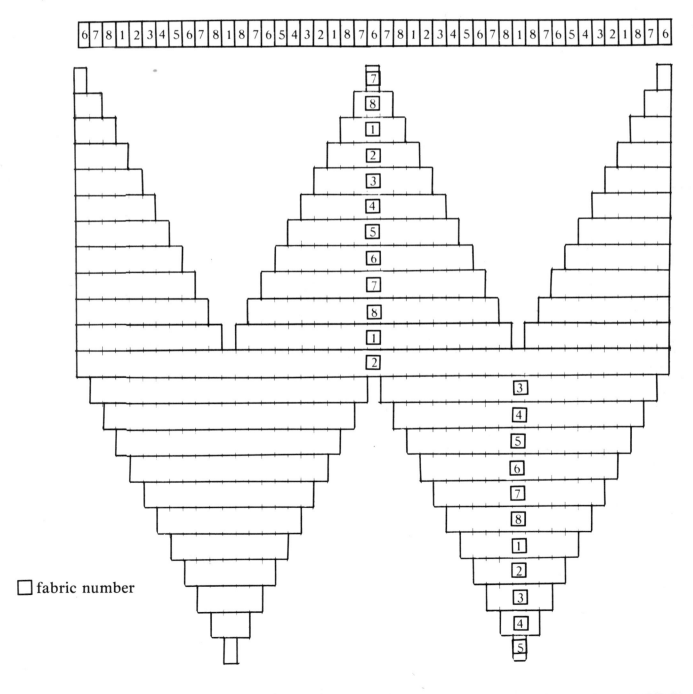

6 7 8 1 2 3 4 5 6 7 8 1 8 7 6 5 4 3 2 1 8 7 6 7 8 1 2 3 4 5 6 7 8 1 8 7 6 5 4 3 2 1 8 7 6

7
8
1
2
3
4
5
6
7
8
1
2

3
4
5
6
7
8
1
2
3
4
5

☐ fabric number

53

Navajo

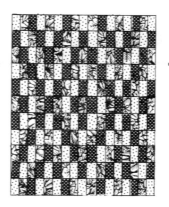

Quilt

King size — 106" × 108"
Rectangle — 2" × 4"

Total rows in sewing layout
(including single row) — 27

Eight fabrics — 1-5/8 yards each
Cut 12 rows of each fabric

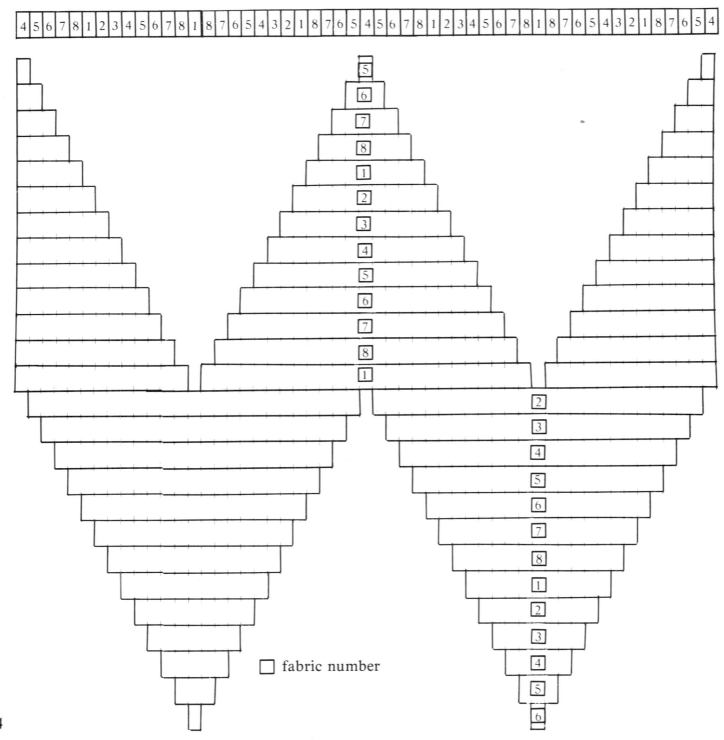

| 4 | 5 | 6 | 7 | 8 | 1 | 2 | 3 | 4 | 5 | 6 | 7 | 8 | 1 | 8 | 7 | 6 | 5 | 4 | 3 | 2 | 1 | 8 | 7 | 6 | 5 | 4 | 5 | 6 | 7 | 8 | 1 | 2 | 3 | 4 | 5 | 6 | 7 | 8 | 1 | 8 | 7 | 6 | 5 | 4 | 3 | 2 | 1 | 8 | 7 | 6 | 5 | 4 |

☐ fabric number

Many Trips Around the World

This quilt is also known as simply *Trip Around the World*. We use the plural version of the name to differentiate this design from the basic *Trip Around the World* quilt. The design forms five diagonal squares. They are separated by fabrics that form a pattern similar to *Double Irish Chain*. The fabric selection and placement is crucial to the design. In order to form the design, the fabrics (except for the last two) should be one color or closely related colors. The last two fabrics should be a contrasting color. For the smaller size, only the last fabric needs to contrast. The fabrics will be used in sequence and then repeated in reverse. The correct fabric placement is printed in boxes on the rows.

Color photographs of Many Trips Around the World quilts are shown on page 66.

Many Trips Around the World

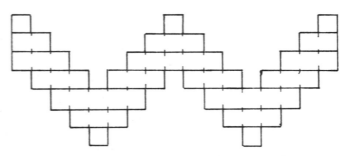

Follow the basic instructions for cutting and sewing the rows.

The *Many Trips Around the World* quilt is made in four sections that are identical and use the same sewing layout. They are connected by single rows of squares that complete the design.

The sewing layout begins with three squares. Each row in the center increases by one square on each side. The rows on the side increase one square on one side only. Continue increasing the rows as the layout indicates. Beginning with one square in the center and one on each side, the rows will then decrease in size.

The sewn rows will duplicate the sewing layout. Press the seams in alternate directions. Carefully place the cut rows face down on each other. Sew them together in the correct order, forming the four sections of the quilt.

Sew the separate squares together to form the five single rows. Follow the fabric numbers carefully, since the fabrics are repeated in reverse sequence. Make three rows with fabric arrangement A, and two rows with fabric arrangement B.

Two of the completed sections must be turned upside down to create the design. The single rows complete the design. Sew the single rows between the sections as diagrammed.

The sewn rows duplicate the sewing layout

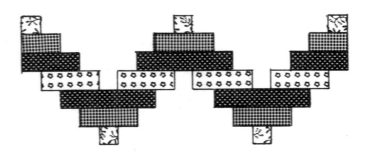

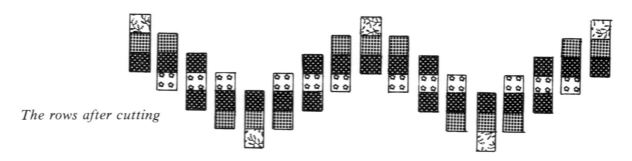

The rows after cutting

The rearranged rows now form the design

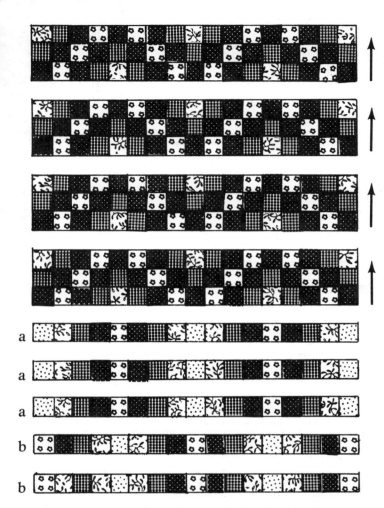

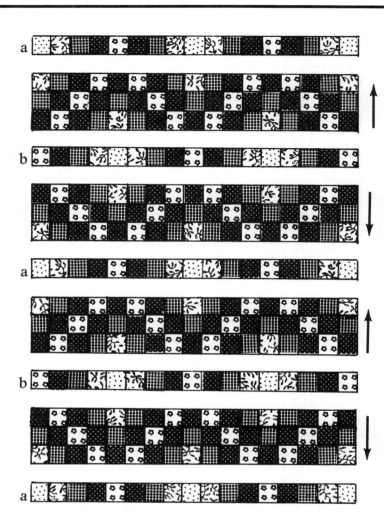

The four identical sections and the five single rows

The second and fourth sections have been turned upside down and the single rows have been inserted between the sections to complete the design.

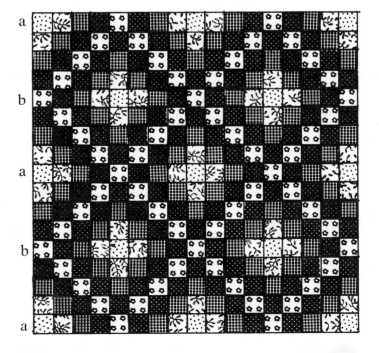

Many Trips Around the World

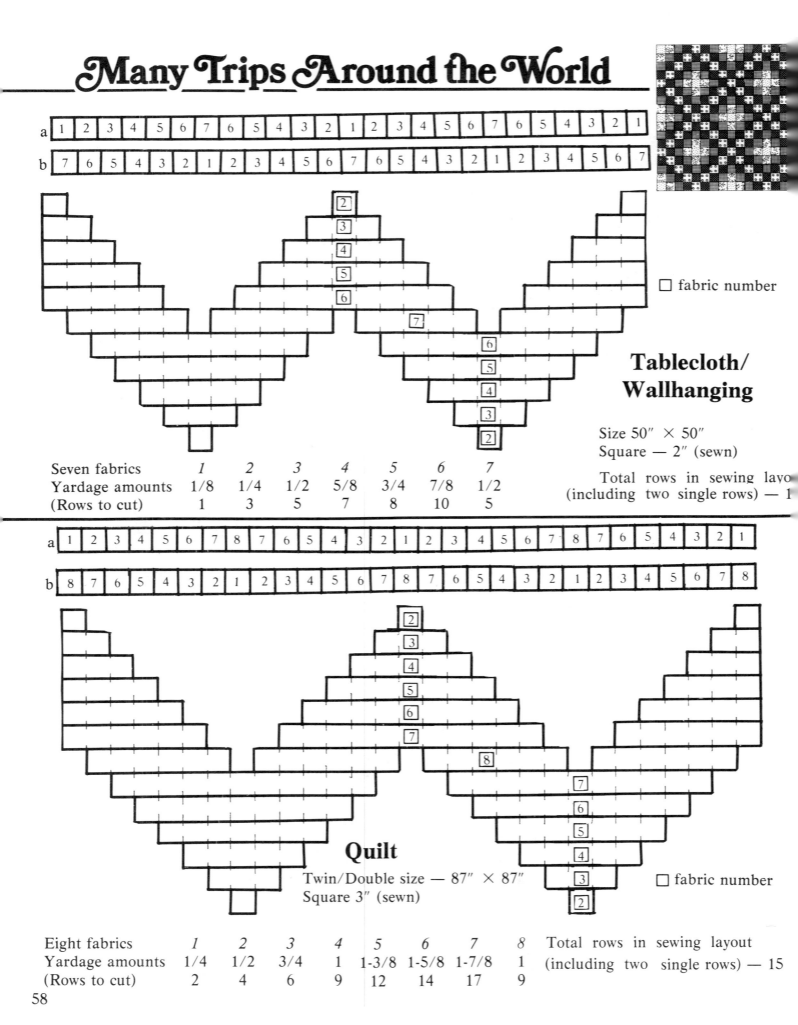

a | 1 | 2 | 3 | 4 | 5 | 6 | 7 | 6 | 5 | 4 | 3 | 2 | 1 | 2 | 3 | 4 | 5 | 6 | 7 | 6 | 5 | 4 | 3 | 2 | 1

b | 7 | 6 | 5 | 4 | 3 | 2 | 1 | 2 | 3 | 4 | 5 | 6 | 7 | 6 | 5 | 4 | 3 | 2 | 1 | 2 | 3 | 4 | 5 | 6 | 7

☐ fabric number

Tablecloth/Wallhanging

Size 50″ × 50″
Square — 2″ (sewn)

Total rows in sewing layo...
(including two single rows) — 1...

Seven fabrics	1	2	3	4	5	6	7
Yardage amounts	1/8	1/4	1/2	5/8	3/4	7/8	1/2
(Rows to cut)	1	3	5	7	8	10	5

a | 1 | 2 | 3 | 4 | 5 | 6 | 7 | 8 | 7 | 6 | 5 | 4 | 3 | 2 | 1 | 2 | 3 | 4 | 5 | 6 | 7 | 8 | 7 | 6 | 5 | 4 | 3 | 2 | 1

b | 8 | 7 | 6 | 5 | 4 | 3 | 2 | 1 | 2 | 3 | 4 | 5 | 6 | 7 | 8 | 7 | 6 | 5 | 4 | 3 | 2 | 1 | 2 | 3 | 4 | 5 | 6 | 7 | 8

Quilt

Twin/Double size — 87″ × 87″
Square 3″ (sewn)

☐ fabric number

Eight fabrics	1	2	3	4	5	6	7	8
Yardage amounts	1/4	1/2	3/4	1	1-3/8	1-5/8	1-7/8	1
(Rows to cut)	2	4	6	9	12	14	17	9

Total rows in sewing layout
(including two single rows) — 15

Many Trips Around the World

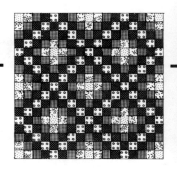

Quilt

Double/Queen — 90″ × 90″
Square — 2″ (sewn)

Twelve fabrics	1	2	3	4	5	6	7	8	9	10	11	12
Yardage amounts	1/8	1/4	1/2	5/8	3/4	7/8	1	1-1/8	1-1/4	1-3/8	1-1/2	7/8
(Rows to cut)	1	3	5	7	8	10	12	14	16	18	20	11

Total rows in the sewing layout (including two single rows) — 23

This is the sewing layout for the quilt on the cover. Some of the fabrics were used twice within the sequence. The same fabric was used for #1 and #12; and #3 and #11 are the same fabric.

a [1 2 3 4 5 6 7 8 9 10 11 12 11 10 9 8 7 6 5 4 3 2 1 2 3 4 5 6 7 8 9 10 11 12 11 10 9 8 7 6 5 4 3 2 1]

b [12 11 10 9 8 7 6 5 4 3 2 1 2 3 4 5 6 7 8 9 10 11 12 11 10 9 8 7 6 5 4 3 2 1 2 3 4 5 6 7 8 9 10 11 12]

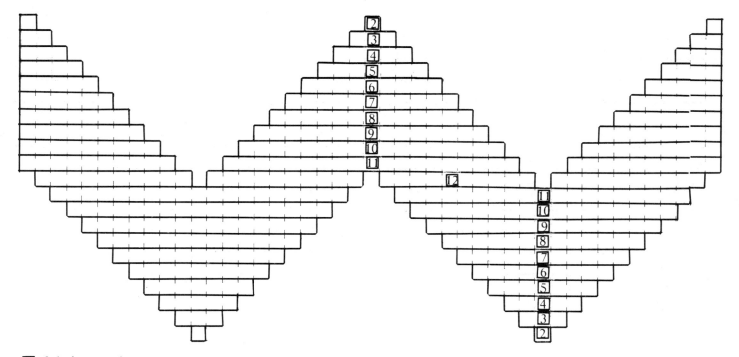

□ fabric number

Many Trips Around the World

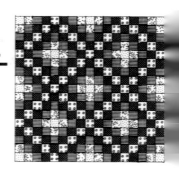

Quilt

Queen/King size — 99″ × 99″
Square — 3″ (sewn)

Nine fabrics	1	2	3	4	5	6	7	8	9
Yardage amounts	1/4	1/2	3/4	1	1-3/8	1-5/8	1-7/8	2-1/8	1 1/4
(Rows to cut)	2	4	6	9	12	14	17	20	11

Total rows in sewing layout
(including two single rows) — 17

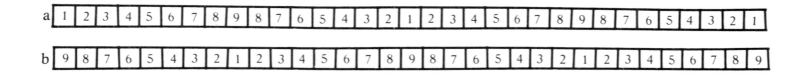

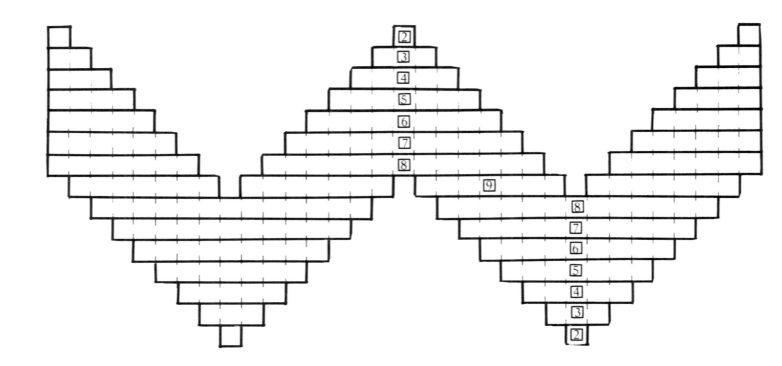

☐ fabric number

Trip Around the World

The fabrics can create a square or rectangular design in the *Trip Around the World* quilt. Each square is on the diagonal. When figuring the size of this quilt, add the diagonal measurement of the squares. The diagonal measurement is larger. This quilt is very attractive on a bed since the design follows the shape of the bed. This design is reinforced by repeating the fabrics in sequence. We list the number of fabrics that can be repeated the same number of times. (If the sewing layout has 21 rows, we use seven fabrics. They will each be repeated three times.) Fabrics can also be repeated in reverse.

Since the squares are on the diagonal, striped fabrics are not recommended for the *Trip Around the World* quilt.

Color photographs of Trip Around the World quilts are shown on pages 68 and 69.

Trip Around the World

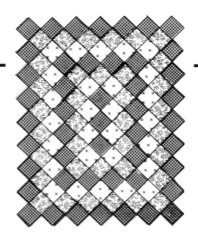

Follow the basic instructions for cutting and sewing the rows.

The *Trip Around the World* quilt is made in three sections; two identical sections and one single row. Each of the two identical sections are half of the quilt, diagonally. On this quilt, the first square of the sewing layout is the same fabric as the center square in the single row. The sections will be offset one square when they are joined. This is the only way to make the design rectangular. For a longer quilt, several single rows can be added. In order to make a square quilt or pillow, the single row will be two squares longer. The fabric sequence will begin at the center square. The layout will begin with the next fabric.

The sewing layout begins with one square. Each row increases by one square on each side until the sewing layout is completed.

These sewn rows will duplicate the sewing layout. When they are cut and resewn, they will form the *Trip Around the World* design. Press the seams in alternate directions before cutting. As the rows are cut apart, they should be placed face down with the top edges even. These cut rows do not contain the same number of squares, as do all the other quilts. When the rows are sewn, the edge of the last square will overlap 1/4 inch.

Sew the separate squares into the single row. Join the three sections, offsetting them one square. The outside squares form a staggered edge. For an unusual finish, bind around the outside squares. For a straight edge, the squares must be trimmed. Staystitch before cutting, since that is the bias of the squares.

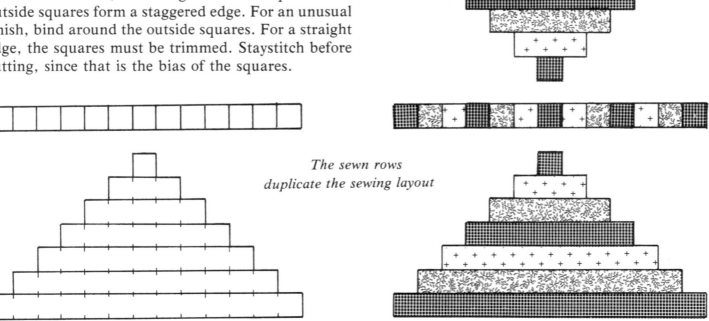

The sewn rows duplicate the sewing layout

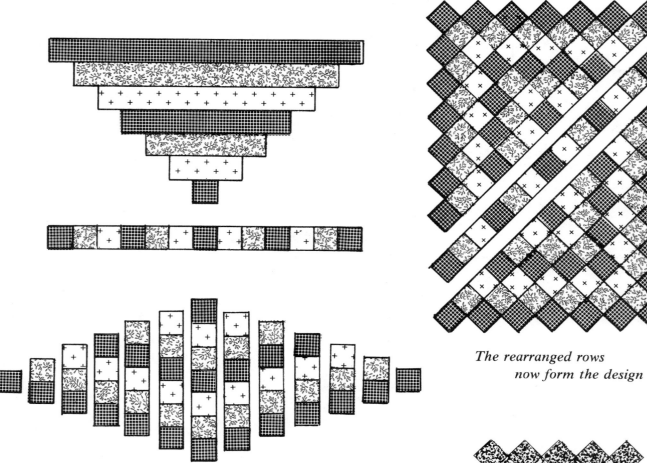

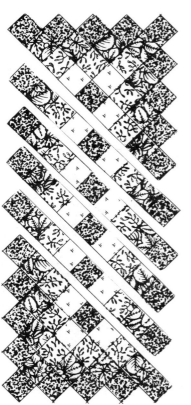

The rearranged rows
now form the design

The rows after cutting

Offset the single rows between
the two sections to form a rectangle.

Trip Around the World

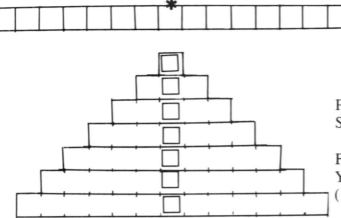

Pillow

Pillow size — 15" × 15"
Square — 1-3/4" (sewn)

Five fabrics	1	2	3	4	5
Yardage amounts	1/4	1/4	1/8	1/8	1/8
(Rows to cut)	2	2	1	1	1

Total rows in sewing layout (including single row) — 7

The single row will extend two squares beyond the two sections to form a square. Fabric sequence begins in the single row. The next fabric is used for the first row of the sewing layout.

Pillow Sham

Sham size 22" × 30"
Square — 2" (sewn)
For two shams —

Seven fabrics	1	2	3	4	5	6	7
Yardage amounts	1/2	1/2	1/4	1/4	1/4	3/8	3/8
(Rows to cut)	5	6	2	3	3	4	4

Seven fabrics — Use fabrics in sequence.

Five fabrics	1	2	3	4	5
Yardage amount	1/2	1/2	1/2	1/2	3/8
(Rows to cut)	6	6	6	6	3

Five fabrics —

Use fabrics in sequence, then repeat fabrics in reverse.

Total rows in sewing layout (including single row) — 10

Make two single rows. Offset each row between the two sections to form a rectangle.

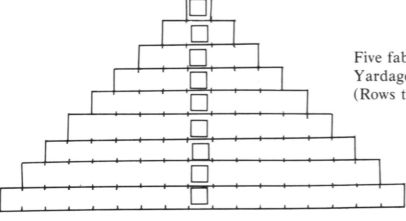

*Begin fabric sequence here.
☐ Write fabric number here.

64

25 (left) *Evening Shadows* (76″ × 94″) by Helen Young. An elongated version of the *Sunshine and Shadow* design, this quilt makes dramatic use of complementary colors.

26 (below) A closer look at some of the different fabrics in the quilt.

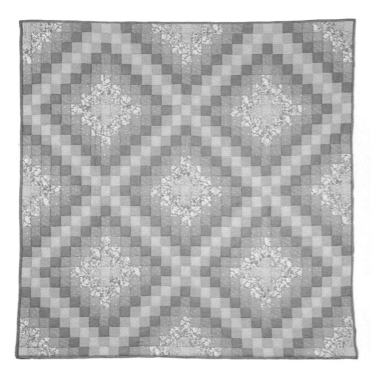

28 (below) *Many Trips Around the World* (99″ × 99″) by Gail Williams. The complementary colors of blue and rust emphasize the diagonal design.

27 (above) *Many Trips Around the World* (99″ × 99″) by Blanche Young. Using two large scale prints together gives a lacy look to this quilt.

29 Ruffled shams add the finishing touch to this *Many Trips Around the World* quilt by Margaret Green.

30 *Trip Around the World* (105″ × 115″) by
Helen Young. This quilt contains eight
fabrics used in the same sequence three
times. The light peach against the dark
brown creates a luminous effect. (Quilt
courtesy of Mr. and Mrs. Bradley Prophet)

31 *Trip Around the World* (90″ × 100″) by
Blanche Young. The fabrics in this quilt are
repeated in reverse sequence. This quilt is
especially effective on a bed because the
design follows the contour of the bed.

32 The soft colors make this *Trip Around the World* tablecloth
an attractive addition to a room. By Blanche Young.

33 (left) *Trip Around the World* (90″ × 100″) by Blanche Young. The pointed edges have been bound rather than trimmed straight. This adds to the character of the quilt.

34 (above) *Trip Around the World*, *Streak of Lightning*, *Sunshine and Shadow* pillows by Blanche Young.

35 (right) The eyelet fabric adds a delicate touch to the *Trip Around the World* quilt and shams by Janet Kappe.

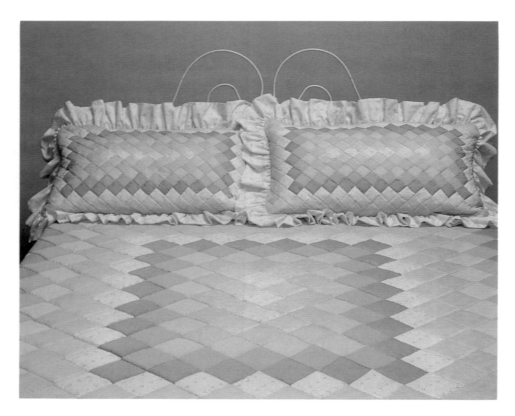

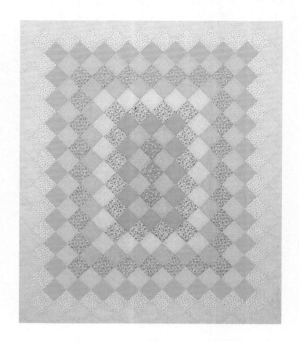

36 One of Melissa's favorite things is her *Trip Around the World* quilt. Quilt and infant seat pad by Helen Young.

37 *Trip Around the World* (85″ × 95″) by Charlotte Beem. The light to dark fabric arrangement creates a balanced design.

38, 39, 40 *Trip Around the World* (39″ × 46″) by the authors.
(top right) Twelve fabrics are used in this crib sized quilt.
(center right) The same twelve fabrics, in reverse order.
(lower right) To achieve this effect, reverse the sequence of seven fabrics within the quilt.

43 (clockwise from top) *Streak of Lightning, Sunshine and Shadow, Trip Around the World* pillows by Helen Young. Pillows are approximately 16 inches square.

42 (above) *Streak of Lightning* pillow and *Many Trips Around the World* wallhanging by Wendy Dodge. Each square in the wallhanging is one half inch. This miniaturized version still effectively displays the design because of careful fabric placement.

41 (opposite) Several different quilt designs are artfully combined in this setting by Wendy Dodge. *Sunshine and Shadow* decorates the magazine rack, fabric box, lampshade, and center pillows. The table is covered with a *Many Trips Around the World* tablecloth. *Trip Around the World* pillows are on the right of the bench. *Streak of Lightning* pillow is on the left of bench.

44 This *Trip Around the World* tablecloth by Betty Poole adds a decorative accent to the home.

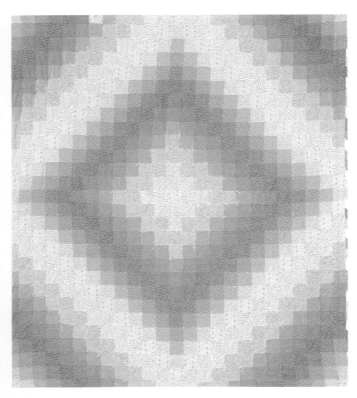

46 *Sunshine and Shadow* (75″ × 81″) by Ginnie Beem. The greens in this tied quilt are accented by the red in one of the prints.

45 (above) This *Sunshine and Shadow* Christmas tablecloth by Betty Poole is highlighted by an embroidered monogram.

47 (right) Festive reds and greens welcome in the holidays in this *Trip Around the World* tablecloth by Charlotte Beem.

Trip Around the World

Tablecloth

Size 52″ × 73″

Square — 2-1/2″ (sewn)

Five fabrics	1	2	3	4	5
Yardage amounts	3/4	7/8	1	1-1/8	1-1/4
(Rows to cut)	7	8	9	10	11

Make five single rows. Offset each row between
the two sections to form a rectangle.

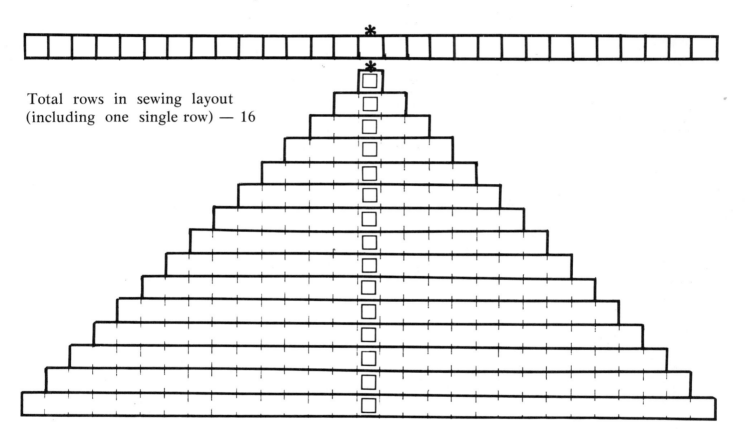

Total rows in sewing layout
(including one single row) — 16

Trip Around the World

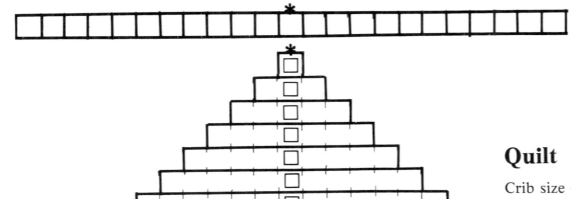

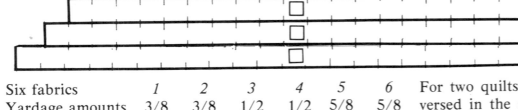

Quilt

Crib size — 39″ × 46″
Square — 2-1/2″ (sewn)

Six fabrics	1	2	3	4	5	6
Yardage amounts	3/8	3/8	1/2	1/2	5/8	5/8
(Rows to cut)	3	3	4	4	5	6

Total rows in sewing layout (including single row) — 13

For two quilts — Fabric sequence will be reversed in the second quilt (see plates 38 and 39).

Twelve fabrics — 1/2 yard each
Cut 4 rows of each fabric

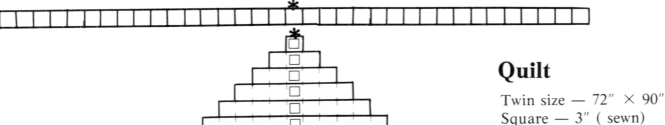

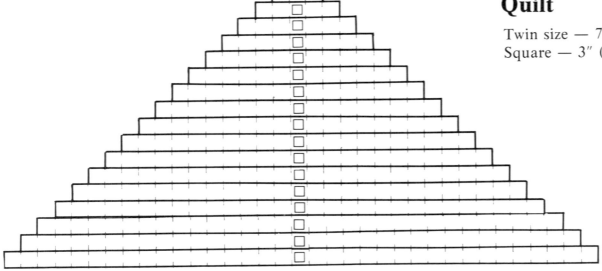

Quilt

Twin size — 72″ × 90″
Square — 3″ (sewn)

Six fabrics	1	2	3	4	5	6
Yardage amounts	7/8	1	1-1/8	1-1/4	1-3/8	1-1/2
(Rows to cut)	7	9	10	11	12	13

Total rows in sewing layout (including one single row) — 19

Make three single rows. Offset each row between the two sections to form a rectangle.

❋ Begin fabric sequence here.
☐ Write fabric number here.

Trip Around the World

Make one single row. Offset the row between the two sections to form a rectangle. Fabric sequence begins in the single row and in the first row of the layout.

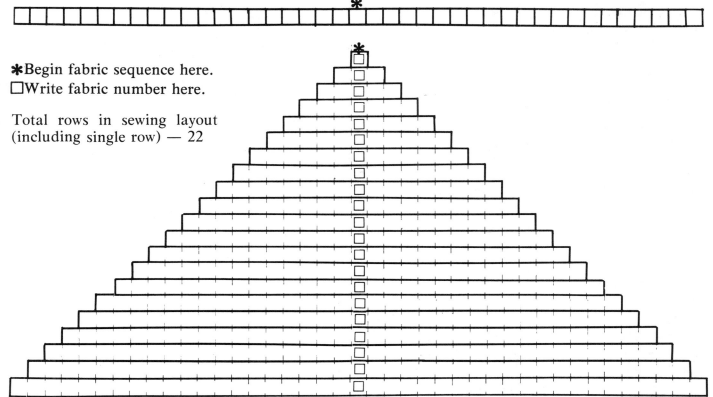

✱ Begin fabric sequence here.
☐ Write fabric number here.

Total rows in sewing layout (including single row) — 22

Quilt

Double/Queen size — 85" × 94"
Square — 3" (sewn)

Seven fabrics	1	2	3	4
Yardage amounts	1-1/8	1-1/4	1-1/4	1-3/8
(Rows to cut)	9	10	11	12

	5	6	7
	1-1/2	1-5/8	1-3/4
	14	15	16

Reverse sequence —
Eleven fabrics — 1 yard each of #1 through #10; 5/8 yard of #11 (Cut 8 rows each of fabrics #1 through #10: cut 4 rows of #11)
Use fabrics in sequence, then repeat fabrics in reverse (see plate 31).

Quilt

King size — 100" × 110"
Square — 3-1/2" (sewn)

Seven fabrics	1	2	3	4
Yardage amounts	1-1/4	1-3/8	1-1/2	1-3/4
(Rows to cut)	10	11	12	14

	5	6	7
	1-7/8	2	2-1/8
	15	16	17

Reverse sequence —
Eleven fabrics — 1-1/8 yard each fabrics #1 through #10; 3/4 yard of #11 (Cut 9 rows each of fabrics #1 through #10; cut 5 rows of #11).
Use fabrics in sequence, then repeat fabrics in reverse (see plate 31).

Finishing the Quilts

Borders

A border, or series of borders, will act as a frame for the quilt design. Borders will also make a quilt larger if necessary. If you would like to add borders but do not need the quilt to be larger, make the smaller size of quilt.

Choose one or more of the fabrics used in the quilt. We try to use the colors in the same proportion they were used in the quilt. Borders will be more interesting if they are different widths. Printed fabrics can be pieced without noticable seams. Plain fabrics will show seam lines.

For mitered corners, cut the borders as long as the quilt plus twice the width of the borders. Sew the different borders for each side together before attaching them to the quilt. The border will need to extend beyond the edge of the quilt the same amount as its width. Attach the borders starting and stopping the stitching 1/4 inch from the edges of the quilt. Lay the quilt flat with the borders crossing. Mark where they intersect. Fold back and crease one border piece. With the crease as a guide, sew up to, but not beyond the other stitching. Cut off the excess fabric.

Squared corners are more traditional with these quilts. Cut the first border the same length as the quilt top. Sew on the top and bottom edges first. Then sew on the side pieces, stopping a few inches from the end. Cut off any excess, allowing for a 1/4 inch seam. Sew the corner square onto the side border, and then continue sewing it to the quilt. Use this technique on each border fabric. Measure to determine the length of the next border. Press the quilt top after the borders are attached.

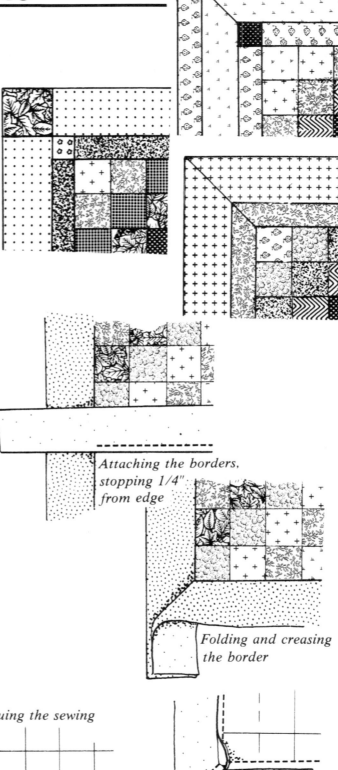

Attaching the borders, stopping 1/4" from edge

Folding and creasing the border

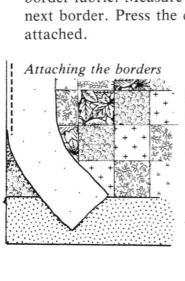

Attaching the borders

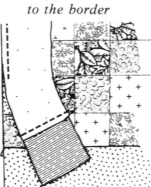

Sewing the corner square to the border

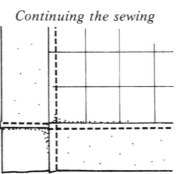

Continuing the sewing

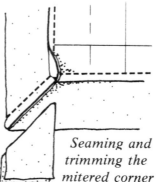

Seaming and trimming the mitered corner

Basting The Quilt

The quilt can be conveniently quilted on a hoop if the three layers have been carefully basted together. Sew the backing pieces together with 3/4 inch seams. Trim off the selvages, then press the seams open. Cut the backing at least two inches larger than the quilt top on all four sides. Cut the batting the same size as the backing.

On the do-it-yourself frame described in the supply list, the backing is thumb-tacked to the boards. Allow two inches of overhang. Carefully spread out the batting on top of the backing. Lay the quilt on top of the batting, smoothing out any fullness. With the edges of the quilt lined up with the edges of the boards, thumb-tack at least every ten inches. The quilt should be smooth but not taut.

With a large embroidery needle threaded with quilting thread, baste the three layers together, stitching on every other row. Baste parallel to the frames as far in as can be reached. Remove the quilt from the frame, and baste the center area on a table.

Basting the quilt on a large table or two tables pushed together, is easy and practical. Some of the quilt will be hanging off the table. Tape the backing to the table to keep it from wrinkling. Carefully spread out the batting on top of the backing. Place the quilt on top of the batting, smoothing out any wrinkles or fullness. Match up the centers of the top and bottom edges. Baste in parallel rows starting in the center.

Basting in parallel rows
matching the centers of the edges

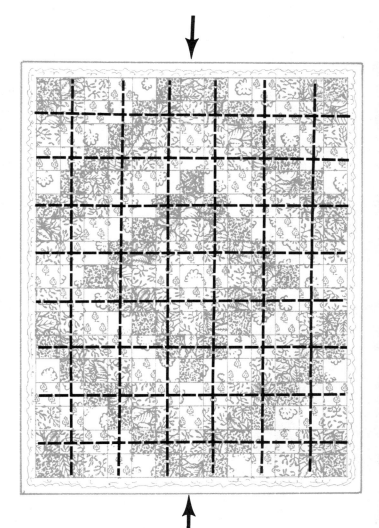

Quilting

Whether the stitching emphasizes the design or simply outlines the squares, the quilting will add another dimension to the design. The stitches themselves are not as important as the effect they create. However, the stitches should be as small, even, and straight as possible. Small stitches are achieved with practice. No amount of practice will result in small stitches if the batting is too thick! It is the quilting that adds to the texture of the quilts' surface, not the thickness of the batting.

If the quilt has been carefully basted, the quilting could almost begin anywhere. We generally begin in the center. We quilt in rows, from edge to edge, working outward. Position the quilt in the hoop so the quilting direction is right to left. The outer hoop should not be tight and the quilt should have some slack.

Thread the needle with 18 inches of quilting thread. Make a small knot in the end. Take a large stitch into the batting and bring the needle up at the starting point. Hide the knot by popping it through the fabric into the batting. Push the needle through the layers with the middle finger. Protect this finger with a thimble. Touch the fingers of the underneath hand with the needle to make sure all the layers have been stitched. Quilting is a running stitch; the needle is at an angle. Put several stitches on the needle at a time. This keeps the stitches straight. To end a row of quilting, tie a knot in the remaining thread. Take a large stitch into the batting, and pop the knot through the fabric.

Thread several needles and quilt on more than one row before moving the hoop. Don't quilt close to the edges of the hoop. The borders will be easier to quilt if a basted strip of fabric extends from the edge of the quilt to the hoop. When the quilting is finished, remove all the basting stitches. The outside edges should now be basted with small stitches so that all three layers can be bound.

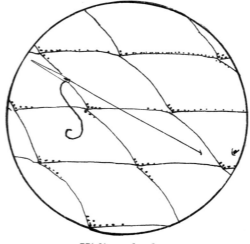

Hiding the knot

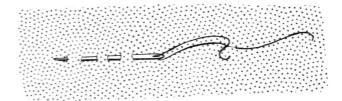

Taking several stitches at a time

Quilting several rows

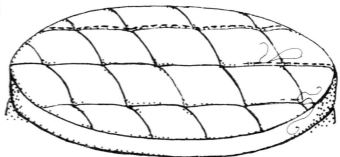

Quilting Designs

Stitching 1/4 inch in from the seam on every square is a traditional way to quilt. Experienced quilters are able to do this without marking the top.

Quilting next to the seams outlines the squares and takes less time than quilting 1/4 inch in. Quilt on the side of the seam without the seam allowance.

Quilting lines can be parallel to the design. This would accentuate the diagonal square design of *Sunshine and Shadow*, and the diamond design of *Evening Shadows*.

Many Amish quilts were quilted diagonally in both directions. The quilting formed an X in each square.

Lines can be marked with a ruler and pencil. Draw lightly with a regular pencil or with a dressmaker's chalk pencil. Mark the quilt top before it is basted to the batting and backing.

The quilting in the borders should correspond to the rest of the quilting.

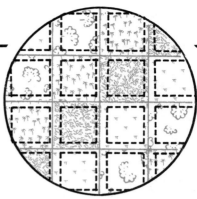

Quilting 1/4" in on each square

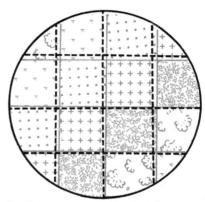

Quilting next to the seams

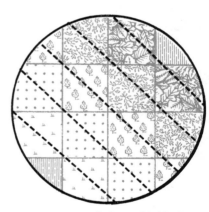

Quilting parallel to the design

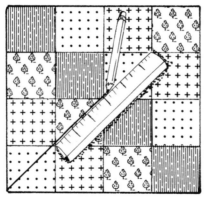

Marking the quilting design

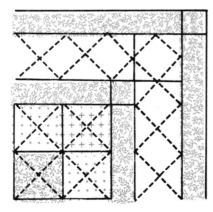

Border quilting designs

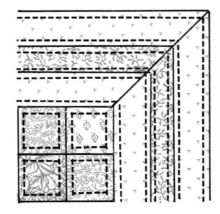

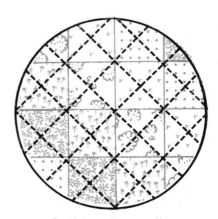

Quilting diagonally

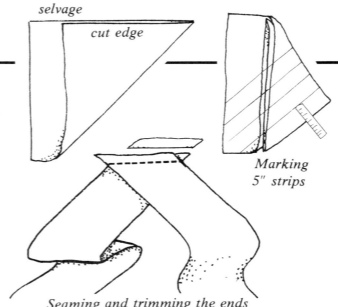

*Marking
5" strips*

Binding The Quilt

The binding finishes the edges and serves as a frame for the quilt. We use a wide, bias, double binding. It is sewn to the quilt on the machine and finished on the back by hand.

Fold the fabric with the cut edge at the selvage to find the true bias. Fold again, with the folds together. Starting at the folded edges measure and mark the fabric into five inch strips. Cut into strips starting with the fold. Sew the strips together with 1/2 inch seams to form one long strip. Trim the seams to 1/4 inch and press them open. Fold the binding in half lengthwise and press. Staystitch the raw edges together, 1/4 inch in, without stretching the binding. Leave six inches open at one end.

With the first six inches left free, sew the binding to all three layers of the quilt starting at the bottom edge. Stop sewing 1/4 inch away from the corner. Backstitch one or two stitches, then raise the needle and presser foot. Make a pleat in the corner to give the finished binding a mitered effect. The pleat should measure 3/4 of an inch. Form the pleat over a 3/4 inch piece of cardboard. Reinsert the needle on the other side of the pleat without leaving a gap. With the needle in, pivot the quilt and resume sewing. Do not sew over the pleat. Continue sewing on the binding, forming a pleat in each corner.

Stop stitching about twelve inches from the starting point. Remove the quilt from the sewing machine. The ends of the binding can be seamed together by removing some of the staystitching. Lay the shorter end of the binding on top of the other piece. Cut the other end, allowing for 1/4 inch seams. Sew the ends together. Fold the binding and finish attaching to the quilt.

Bring the folded edge of the binding to the back of the quilt. Trim off any excess backing fabric but leave any batting. Extra batting can be used to pad the binding. Pin, then slipstitch the binding to the quilt.

To bind the pointed edges of the *Trip Around the World* quilt, cut the strips 2-1/2 inches wide. There will be a 1/4 inch pleat on the outside corner of every square. The inside corner does not have a pleat; instead, it should be clipped 1/4 inch. Sew to the inside corner and lift the presser foot, leaving the needle in the fabric. Pivot the quilt and resume sewing. Slipstitch the back of the binding to the quilt.

Seaming and trimming the ends

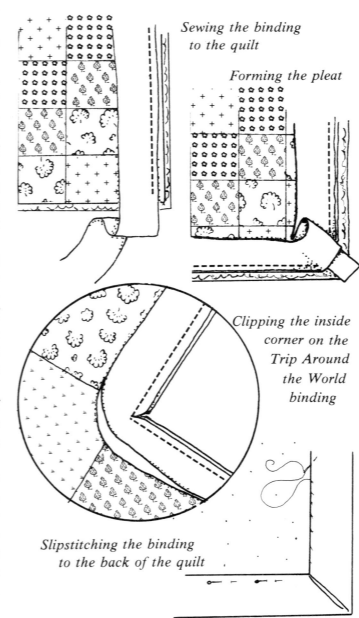

*Sewing the binding
to the quilt*

Forming the pleat

*Clipping the inside
corner on the
Trip Around
the World
binding*

*Slipstitching the binding
to the back of the quilt*

Finishing the Smaller Projects

Baby Quilts

The prairie points edging is a delightful finish for a crib quilt. Cut 4 inch squares. Fold them in half diagonally and press. Fold them again and press. They are tucked inside each other and then pinned to the edge of the quilt top. Adjust them to fit at the corners. Sew them to the quilt, including all the raw edges in the seam. The quilt is then basted together for quilting or tying.

Eyelet ruffles are also sewn on before the quilt is basted. Sew the eyelet to the quilt top, allowing extra gathers in the corners, and overlapping the ends.

Tying is an ideal way to finish a quilt for a child. Tying with yarn is decorative and very practical. The ties can withstand many launderings. Use a washable yarn in the color or colors of the quilt. The quilt in plate 4 has been tied with yellow yarn on the yellow fabrics, and with blue on the blue fabrics.

Thread a small darning needle with a double strand of yarn. Take one stitch through the three layers of the quilt. Tie a square knot. Tie several knots in a row, then clip the yarn. Trim the ties to about one inch in length.

After the quilt is tied, slipstitch the backing fabric to the back of the prairie points or the ruffle.

Tablecloths

Patchwork can be used throughout the home, instead of just in the bedroom. A patchwork tablecloth will brighten any room. Some of the tablecloths in the color plates have been quilted and bound. Use flannel or very thin batting. The binding should also be very narrow and flat.

Tablecloths can also be simply lined. Cut the backing the same size and sew with right sides together. Leave an opening for turning. Close by slipstitching.

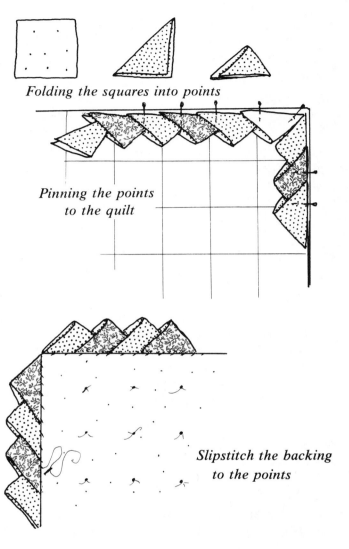

Folding the squares into points

Pinning the points to the quilt

Slipstitch the backing to the points

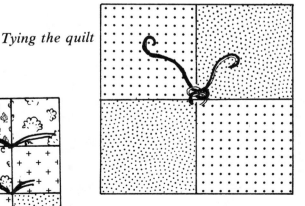

Tying the quilt

Clip and trim the yarn

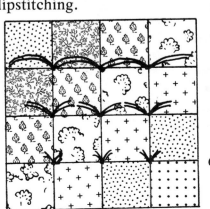

Pillows

Finish the pillows with piping for a tailored look. Use purchased piping, or make your own by cutting bias strips wide enough to cover a cording, plus seams. Using a zipper foot, stitch next to the cording. Sew the piping to the front of the pillow. Corners should be slightly rounded. Clip the seam allowance at the corners. Finish the ends of the piping by opening one end and overlapping the fabric.

Ruffles are also an attractive way to edge the pillows. Cut the ruffles twice their finished width, plus 1/4 inch seam allowances. The length of the ruffle should be 2-1/2 times the distance around the pillow. Seam the ruffle pieces together, then press them in half lengthwise. Using a zig-zag stitch over string is an easy way to make gathers. Simply pull the string to gather the fabric. Position the ruffle on the pillow front, evenly distributing the gathers. Sew to the pillow, rounding the corners slightly. Double ruffles can be gathered together.

Cut the pillow backing 1/2 inch larger than the front. After attaching the piping or ruffles, pin the backing to the pillow. Sew with the backing on the bottom and follow the previous stitching. Leave one side open for turning and stuffing. Close by slip-stitching.

Cut two pieces of backing for each pillow sham. The shams are approximately 22" × 30". Cut two 22" × 22" pieces for the back. These will overlap and form a covered opening. Hem the edges that overlap.

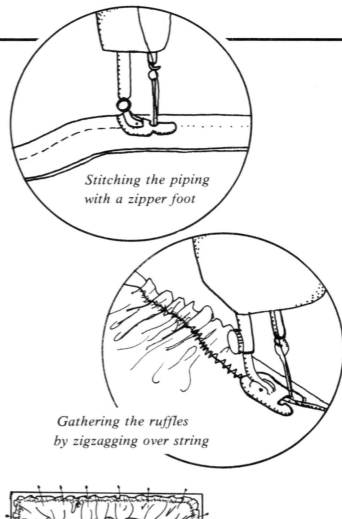

Stitching the piping with a zipper foot

Gathering the ruffles by zigzagging over string

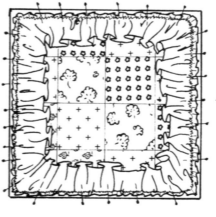

Positioning the ruffles

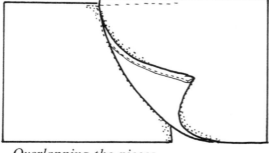

Overlapping the pieces to form a covered opening

Following the previous stitching

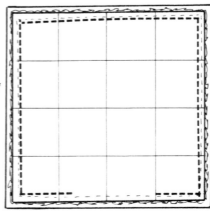

82

Yardage Charts

Fabric amounts are based on 42-43″ wide fabric (45″ wide fabric minus selvages). Some allowance is made for shrinkage.

Measure the quilt top before cutting the backing fabric. Allow at least two inches extra on all sides.

Borders

The length of the quilt will yield 10″ borders (without piecing)

Half the length of the quilt will yield 5″ borders (pieced once on each side)

	Without piecing	Pieced
Twin	2-3/4 yards	1-3/8 yards
Double/Queen	2-7/8 yards	1-1/2 yards
King	3-1/4 yards	1-5/8 yards

Binding

Quilts —	
Crib	1 yard
Twin	1-1/4 yards
Double/Queen	1-1/2 yards
King	1-3/4 yards
Tablecloths	1-1/4 yards

Backing

Backing fabric can be solid color or one of the prints in the quilt.

Pillow (2)	1/2 yard
Shams (2)	1-1/4 yards
Quilts —	
Crib	1-1/2 yards
Twin	5-1/2 yards (2 — 97″ lengths)
Double/Queen	8-3/4 yards (3 — 104″ lengths)
King	9-1/2 yards (3— 114″ lengths)

(Use king size backing amount for double/queen Navajo)

Tablecloth (52″ × 52″)	3-1/4 yards (2 — 58″ lengths)
Tablecloth (63″ × 63″)	3-3/4 yards (2 — 67″ lengths)
Tablecloth (52″ × 73″)	4-1/4 yards (2 — 76″ lengths)

Edging for Crib quilts

Prairie points	1/4 yard each	96 squares total (seven fabrics)
Pre-gathered eyelet	6 yards	

Ruffles

Pillows	5/8 yard	3″ finished (cut 6-1/2″ wide)
	1/2 yard	2-1/2″ finished (cut 5-1/2″ wide)
Pre-gathered eyelet	1-1/2 yards	
Shams (1)	1-1/2 yards	4″ finished (cut 8-1/2″ wide)

This is an easy way to figure yardage for these quilts. No multiplying is involved, only adding. To do your own chart, first determine how many squares (or rectangles) will fit across the width of the fabric. Fabrics that are 45" wide should be figured as 42". Example: A square that is 3-1/2" finished is cut 4". A 4" square will fit ten times across the fabric. Every 4" of fabric will yield 10 squares.

Arrange the numbers in columns. Find the needed number of squares then refer to the first column to instantly convert the total into the number of rows to mark. The middle column tells how much fabric to buy. Whenever we figure yardage this way, we always allow ourselves two extra rows per fabric.

Remember that fabrics are sold by the divisions on a yardstick.

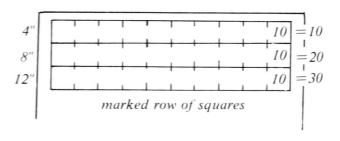

marked row of squares

4-1/2" — 1/8 yard	31-1/2"— 7/8 yard	
9 — 1/4	36 — 1	
13-1/2 — 3/8	40-1/2 — 1 1/8	
18 — 1/2	45 — 1-1/4	
22-1/2 — 5/8	49-1/2 — 1-3/8	
27 — 3/4	54 — 1-1/2	

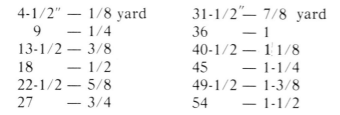

Rectangle size — 2-1/2" × 4-1/2" cut/ 2" × 4" sewn			Square size — 2-1/4" cut/1-3/4" sewn		
Rows	Inches	Total Rectangles	Rows	Inches	Total Squares
1	4-1/2	17	1	2-1/4	19
2	9	34	2	4-1/2	38
3	13-1/2	51	3	6-3/4	57
4	18	68	4	9	76
5	22-1/2	85	5	11-1/4	95
6	27	102	6	13-1/2	114
7	31-1/2	119	7	15-3/4	133
8	36	136	8	18	152
9	40-1/2	153			
10	45	170			
11	49-1/2	187			
12	54	204			

Square size — 2-1/2" cut/2" sewn		
Rows	Inches	Total Squares
1	2-1/2	17
2	5	34
3	7-1/2	51
4	10	68
5	12-1/2	85
6	15	102
7	17-1/2	119
8	20	136
9	22-1/2	153
10	25	170
11	27-1/2	187
12	30	204
13	32-1/2	221
14	35	238
15	37-1/2	255
16	40	272
17	42-1/2	289
18	45	306
19	47-1/2	323
20	50	340
21	52-1/2	357
22	55	374
23	57-1/2	408

Square size — 3-1/2" cut/3" sewn		
Rows	Inches	Total Squares
1	3-1/2	12
2	7	24
3	10-1/2	36
4	14	48
5	17-1/2	60
6	21	72
7	24-1/2	84
8	28	96
9	31-1/2	108
10	35	120
11	38-1/2	132
12	42	144
13	45-1/2	156
14	49	168
15	52-1/2	180
16	56	192
17	59-1/2	204
18	63	216
19	66-1/2	228
20	70	240
21	73-1/2	252

Square size — 3" cut/2-1/2" sewn		
Rows	Inches	Total Squares
1	3	14
2	6	28
3	9	42
4	12	56
5	15	70
6	18	84
7	21	98
8	24	112
9	27	126
10	30	140
11	33	154
12	36	168

Square size — 4" cut/3-1/2" sewn		
Rows	Inches	Total Squares
1	4	10
2	8	20
3	12	30
4	16	40
5	20	50
6	24	60
7	28	70
8	32	80
9	36	90
10	40	100
11	44	110
12	48	120
13	52	130
14	56	140
15	60	150
16	64	160
17	68	170
18	72	180

Charting Different Sizes

The sizes of the quilts can be altered by using a different size of square for the same layout. For example, the *Many Trips Around the World* tablecloth sewing layout was used for the miniature wallhanging in plate 42. The tablecloth was made with 2″ squares, the wallhanging was made with 1/2 inch squares.

To figure how the size would change you will need to know how many squares there are on the edges of the quilt. Simply divide the size of the square into the quilt's measurements. (Example: The square is 3″, the quilt measures 87″ × 99″ — the quilt is 29 × 33 squares.) To enlarge the quilt, use a 3-1/4″ or 3-1/2″ square. (3-1/4″ × 29 squares = 94 1/4″/3-1/4″ × 33 squares = 107-1/4″.) To reduce the size of the quilt use a smaller square. This is the simplest way to change the size of the quilt.

These quilts can also be charted for different sizes or with different sizes of squares. Always figure the sewn measurement of the square. Here are some basic steps to follow: Decide on the approximate measurements of the quilt. Choose the size of square. Divide the size of the square into the measurements of the quilt. This will be the number of squares on the edges.

The *Sunshine and Shadow*, *Evening Shadows*, *Navajo*, and *Many Trips Around the World* quilts must have an odd number of blocks for the design to be centered. Adjust the number of squares or the size of the quilt to have an odd number of squares for these quilts.

Mark of the number of squares on the graph paper with dotted lines. This is the finished size of the quilt.

Streak of Lightning
Chart the layout with the rows increasing on one side until the width of the quilt is reached (at the dotted line). Rows are added until the length is reached (at the dotted line). The rows will then decrease one square on the opposite side.

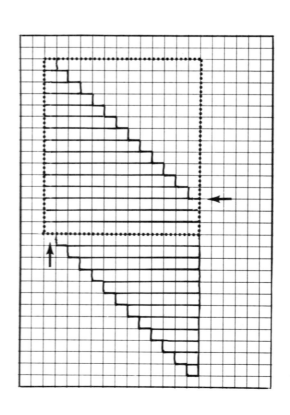

Sunshine and Shadow and Evening Shadows

The single row will extend from edge to edge. Begin to chart the layout below that row. The rows cannot extend beyond the dotted lines. The rows will increase until they reach the width of the quilt. They will decrease when the length is reached (at the dotted line).

Trip Around the World

Decide on the size of the quilt. Choose the size of square, considering its diagonal measurement. Simply draw the square on graph paper and measure it on the diagonal. Divide the diagonal measurement into the width of the quilt to find the number of rows in the layout. Adjust the size of the square or the size of the quilt to arrive at the number of rows you need.

We try to use the number of rows that can be divided by 3, 4, or 5. Then our fabrics will be used in complete sequence 3, 4, or 5 times. For example, with 15 rows, five fabrics can each be used 3 times. With 20 rows, five fabrics will be used 4 times. The length is adjusted by using additional single rows.

Navajo

This design is formed by using a certain number of fabrics. The design will change as additional rows are added. More fabrics must be used to keep the design centered. We recommend changing the size of the rectangle instead of altering the sewing layout.

Many Trips Around the World

This design is also formed with a certain number of fabrics. As rows are added to the sewing layout, additional fabrics must be used. We recommend using a different square instead of changing the layout. Borders can be added to make the quilt larger or rectangular.

Yardage amounts are figured by adding how many squares are on each row of the sewing layout. Line up the total number of squares for each row under the fabric numbers. The yardage charts convert the number of squares into the number of rows to mark and the amount of fabric needed.

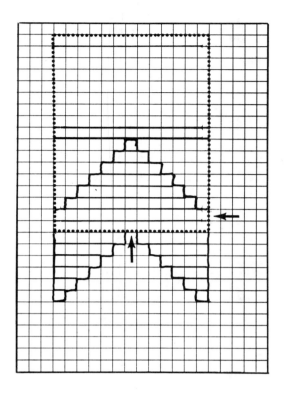

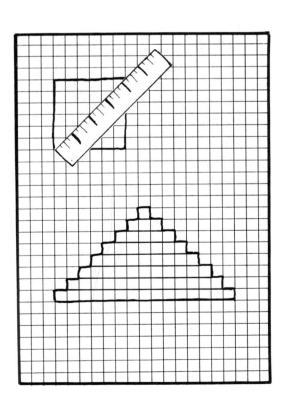

Bibliography

Birren Faber. *Principles of Color.* New York: Van Nostrand Reinhold Company, 1969.

Bishop, Robert. *New Discoveries in American Quilts.* New York: E.P. Dutton & Company, Inc., 1975.

_____, and Elizabeth Safanda. *A Gallery of Amish Quilts.* New York: E.P. Dutton & Company, Inc., 1976.

Gutcheon, Beth, and Jeffrey Gutcheon. *The Quilt Design Workbook.* New York: Rawson Associates Publishers, Inc., 1976.

Holstein, Jonathan. *The Pieced Quilt.* Greenwi[ ] Connecticut: New York Graphic Society, L[ ] 1973.

James, Michael. *The Quiltmaker's Handbook.* En[ ] wood Cliffs, New Jersey: Prentice-Hall, Inc., 19[ ]

Leone, Diana. *The Sampler Quilt.* Santa Clara, C[ ] fornia: Leone Publications, 1980.

Orlofsky, Patsy, and Myron Orlofsky. *Quilts in Am[ ] ica.* New York: McGraw-Hill Book Company, 19[ ]

Puckett, Marjorie, and Gail Giberson. *Prima[ ] Patchwork.* Redlands, California: Cabin Cr[ ] 1975.

About the Authors

Blanche Young is the innovator of the methods in this book. She began making quilts using traditional methods, completing her first quilt at age thirteen. She always sewed for herself and family but her quiltmaking endeavors were interrupted by other events. (A quilt begun for her first baby was not finished until after the birth of her seventh!)

She has taught sewing since 1940 and has worked for all the major sewing machine companies. She began teaching quiltmaking in 1971. Combining the traditional aspects of quiltmaking with her sewing machine skills resulted in the techniques in this book.

Blanche lives in Westminster, California with her husband, Dallas. She has three grandsons and three granddaughters. The youngest, Heather, models the quilt in plate 13.

Growing up in a home filled with fabrics and quilts, it was almost inevitable that Helen Young would become a quilter. She has taught quiltmaking since 1975. This shared interest has enabled daughter and mother to work together in the development of the techniques in this book and in their first book, *The Lone Star Quilt Handbook.* They differ in color preferences and on some technical details. (Helen makes pink quilts and can quilt without a thimble.)

She loves antique needlework and collects 18th and 19th century cross-stitch samplers, handmade laces and, of course, quilts.